Very Vegan Christmas Cookies

Very Vegan Christmas Cookies

Ellen Brown

CIDER MILL PRESS

BOOK PUBLISHERS

Kennebunkport, Maine

Cider Mill Press Book Publishers
"Where good books are ready for press"
12 Port Farm Road
Kennebunkport, Maine 04046

Visit us on the Web!
www.cidermillpress.com

Design by Alicia Freile, Tango Media
Typeset by Gwen Galeone
Typography: Chaparral Pro, Helvetica Neue, and Latino Rumba
Photos copyright: Page 5, sandra zuerlein; Page 9, Anna Hoychuk; Page 12, Ildi Papp; Page 13, B Calkins; Page 14, AM-STUDiO; Page 15, Shebeko; Page 15, Morgan Lane Photography; Page 17, David P. Smith; Page 17, Coprid; Page 18 (top), Darren Brode; Page 19, Elena Schweitzer; Page 20, Komar Maria; Page 23, hd connelly; Page 24, Elke Dennis; Page 27, Boris Franz; Page 30, katielittle; Page 31, Marcel Paschertz; Page 32, AGfoto; Page 35, Ruth Black; Page 36, sarsmis; Page 39, RoJo Images; Page 40, viennetta; Page 43, Elke Dennis; Page 44, viennetta; Page 47, Glenn Price; Page 48, kentoh; Page 51, Antonino D'Anna; Page 52, Elena Elisseeva; Page 55, Lilyana Vynogradova; Page 56, Glenn Price; Page 59, David P. Smith; Page 60, maxfeld; Page 65, finaeva_i; Page 66, Andrea Skjold; Page 69, Catherine Murray; Page 70, Kostia; Page 73, AGfoto; Page 74, John Kasawa; Page 77, hxdbzxy; Page 78, barbaradudzinska; Page 81, Nattika; Page 82, tacar; Page 85, Drozdowski; Page 86, 29september; Page 90, sarsmis; Page 93, Nicoleta Raftu; Page 97, Ev Thomas; Page 98, Carlos Restrepo; Page 101, Madlen; Page 102, 54613; Page 105, DelaLane Photography; Page 110, Elena Elisseeva; Page 113, Tamelina; Page 114, ScriptX; Page 117, Kellis; Page 118, CGissemann; Page 121, Patrick Krabeepetcharat; Page 122, keko64. All used under license from Shutterstock.com

Other photos copyright: Page 89, istockphoto/lvenks; Page 106, istockphoto/Watcha; Page 109, istockphoto/ivanmateev; Page 125, istockphoto/ghutka.

Printed in China

1 2 3 4 5 6 7 8 9 0
First Edition

Contents

Introduction

Everyone loves a good cookie, at any time of the year. But if Thanksgiving is the holiday that "owns" pies, then Christmas is the one most closely associated with cookies. Cookies in fanciful shapes frosted with colored icing and candies along with gingerbread "people" take center stage, but there's a whole pantheon of luscious treats that are the supporting players. There are cookies rolled in confectioners' sugar to look like the snowballs of winter, and rich brownies too.

However, two of the key ingredients in most cookie recipes—butter and eggs—are inconsistent with the vegan lifestyle. *Very Vegan Christmas Cookies* is here to come to your rescue. First and foremost, these cookies are yummy. They're filled with flavorful ingredients, aromatic with spices and citrus zests, and truly decadently delicious. Everyone, regardless of their dietary prohibitions, can eat them!

The choice of a vegan lifestyle, which eschews all animal products in all aspects of life, has been frequently incorrectly described in the popular media as a religion. There is no such thing as vegan theology, although there are strongly held ethical beliefs. There are no metaphysical beliefs or creeds exposed by those choosing to not eat animal products or use animal products in their clothing or other aspects of their life. There are no vegan places of worship, nor are there vegan holidays to celebrate.

There are probably as many unique reasons why people choose a vegan lifestyle as there are vegans in North America. Vegans, now numbering 1 million, are a growing subset of the 7.3 million people who describe themselves as vegetarians, according to a 2008 study conducted by Harris Interactive for *The Vegetarian Times*. Most of the reasons can be categorized into health, animal rights, and concern about the planet's future resources.

Being a vegan is all about conforming to an ethical lifestyle, and about a third of vegans are also practicing Christians. Veganism is another manifestation of spirituality, but they overlay those beliefs onto the tenets of the religion.

While we tend to think of vegetarianism in general and veganism in particular as "modern," it has actually been around longer than Christianity. Kerry S. Walters and Lisa Portmess wrote in their book *Ethical Vegetarianism* that the Greek philosopher Pythagoras was a believer in the transmigration of souls and warned that eating an animal might actually involve the eating of a human soul and should be avoided.

It was during the nineteenth century that vegetarianism as a way of life really established a beachhead in the West, although followers of some sects of Buddhism and Hinduism advocated vegetarianism for centuries because they believed that humans should not inflict pain on other animals.

The first vegetarian society was formed in 1847 in England, and in 1850 Rev. Sylvester Graham, a Presbyterian minister and inventor of the graham cracker, founded the American Vegetarian Society. It was almost a full century later that Donald Watson, a British woodworker, coined the term *vegan*. In 1944 he wrote that while many vegetarians ate dairy and eggs, vegans would not. In 1951 the British Vegan Society defined *veganism* as the "doctrine that man should live without exploiting animals." When the American Vegan Society was formed in 1960, its founder, H. Jay Dinshah, linked veganism to the Jain concept of *ahimsa*, the avoidance of violence against living things.

The most common misconception regarding the vegan diet is that there are such strict limits on what can be eaten that a vegan diet is not nutritionally sound. Both the American Dietetic Association and its Canadian equivalent, as well as the World Health Organization, have endorsed veganism for people of all age groups. After all, the vegan diet includes whole grains, fruits, vegetables, nuts, seeds, and legumes. All of these foods are now emphasized around the world as ones that should be the foundation of a healthy diet.

Plant foods contain eight amino acids, similar to what is found in animal foods but in different amounts. Nuts and soy foods contain complete proteins, which is why so many of the recipes in this book list them as ingredients. Soy and dried figs are also excellent sources of calcium, as are other soy products. The recipes in *Very Vegan Christmas Cookies* were formulated for their flavor, but particular attention was paid to ensuring that these tempting treats are not only strictly vegan but add nutrients to the diet too.

So feel good about baking these cookies, because everyone you bake them for will thank you.

Happy baking!

Ellen Brown
Providence, Rhode Island

CHAPTER 1:

Very Vegan Baking

While cooking is an art, it's science class that takes precedence when it comes to baking. In fact, learning about the properties of ingredients is called food chemistry in any number of culinary schools. Each ingredient in a recipe fulfills a role and functions in a different way. When making vegan baked goods, even cookies, these ingredients change, and knowing the whys and hows of ingredients leads to more delicious results.

In this chapter you'll learn all about vegan ingredients and get some pointers on baking in general and cookies in particular. The chapter ends with some easy icing recipes to dress up your very vegan Christmas cookies.

Vegan Ingredients and How to Use Them Successfully

The two categories of ingredients that must be avoided in vegan baking are dairy products and eggs. Then there are some minor ingredients such as honey that must be substituted in vegan recipes. Here is a guide to vegan versions of ingredients found in traditional cookie recipes:

Butter: This is perhaps the easiest substitution because there are many soy margarines on the market. Margarine will give the cookies a traditional "buttery" flavor. But if the butter is to be melted to make the cookie dough you may consider using vegetable oil. Oil is also very good in cookie recipes that contain a lot of spices. When using oil in place of melted butter, reduce the amount by 10 percent to compensate for the air churned into butter or margarine.

Milk, cream, and buttermilk: I find that plain, full-fat soy milk is the best substitute for cow's milk, and an alternative is rice milk. I tend to shy away from almond milk or coconut milk unless I want that flavor in the cookie. If a recipe calls for heavy cream, use plain soy milk and substitute 3 tablespoons of melted soy margarine for 3 tablespoons of the milk to replicate the butter fat content. To make a soy version of buttermilk, add 2 tablespoons of freshly squeezed lemon juice to each cup of soy milk. Allow the mixture to sit for 10 minutes.

Honey: Honey is a natural sweetener with a distinctive flavor, and I found that pure maple syrup accomplishes the same goal in recipes. Other thick liquids on the list approved for vegans are corn syrup and agave nectar. Corn syrup can be used as it comes from the bottle, but I recommend reducing maple syrup and agave nectar by one-fourth to replicate the viscosity of honey.

No Longer Essential Eggs

There are not one or two substitutes for eggs in vegan baking, there are many because eggs play different roles in baked goods. Eggs add moisture to doughs and batters; each egg is ¼ cup of liquid. But eggs do more than moisten. They also act as a binding agent that holds cookies together as the proteins in them solidify during the baking process, and they act as natural leavening agents that help food to rise.

Cookies are the easiest form of baked good to transform deliciously into vegan fare. They call for very few eggs, and the role of the eggs is most often to provide moisture. However, do not attempt to make a vegan version of any baked good that requires egg whites to be beaten stiffly, such as angel food cakes or meringues. At the present time there is not an egg substitute up to the task of creating that structure.

The product used most often in this book is egg replacement powder, which is marketed under the name Ener-G. It's primarily a combination of potato starch and tapioca starch with a bit of leavening added. The formulation is 1½ teaspoons powder and 2 tablespoons cold water equals 1 egg.

Applesauce is commonly used in vegan recipes as a substitute for the moisture that would have been provided by eggs.

Ground flax seed can be used as a binding agent as a substitute for eggs.

Here are some ingredients that can be substituted for eggs:

• **To give moisture:** Substitute ¼ cup unsweetened smooth applesauce, silken tofu, mashed banana, mashed sweet potato, or soy yogurt.
• **As a binding agent:** Substitute 1 tablespoon of ground flax seed mixed with 3 tablespoons cold water, 2 tablespoons cornstarch or arrowroot mixed with 2 tablespoons cold water, or 2 tablespoons all-purpose flour mixed with ½ teaspoon baking powder and 1 tablespoon water.

Careful "Creaming"

Although there are no dairy products involved in vegan cooking we still refer to the vital step of beating margarine and sugar as "creaming." During this process air is beaten in and is trapped in the margarine's crystalline structure. It is the number and size of the air bubbles (which then become enlarged by the carbon dioxide produced by baking soda or baking powder) that leavens a dough or batter to produce a high, finely-textured product.

The starting point in proper creaming is to ensure that the margarine is at the correct temperature, approximately 70°F. Remove it from the refrigerator and cut each stick into approximately 30 thin slices. Allow them to sit at room temperature for 15 to 20 minutes to soften.

Begin the process by beating the margarine and sugar at low speed to get them blended. Then increase the speed to high, and scrape the bowl frequently. When properly creamed, the texture of the butter and sugar mixture will be light and fluffy.

Chocolate Creations

Of course chocolate and cocoa powder, which come from the pods of a cocoa tree, are vegan. But with chocolate of a lesser quality many additives can be used in the processing that contain milk solids or milk fat. So do be careful when choosing a brand to get one with a high chocolate content, pure ingredients, and—most importantly—no additives. In the past few years a vegan version of "milk" chocolate has also appeared on the market, but it remains relatively difficult to find.

The key to the success for all chocolate desserts is to use a high-quality product and the one that is specified in the recipe. Here's a quick guide to chocolate:

• **Unsweetened.** Also referred to as baking or bitter chocolate, this is the purest of all cooking chocolate. It is hardened chocolate liquor (the essence of the cocoa bean, not an alcohol) that contains no sugar. It is usually packaged in a bar of 8 (1-ounce) blocks. According to the U.S. standard of identity, unsweetened chocolate must contain 50 to 58 percent cocoa butter.
• **Bittersweet.** This chocolate is slightly sweetened with sugar, and the amount varies depending on the manufacturer. This chocolate must contain 35 percent chocolate liquor and should be used when intense chocolate flavor is desired. Also use it interchangeably with semisweet chocolate in cooking and baking.
• **Semisweet.** This chocolate is sweetened with sugar, but unlike bittersweet, it also can have added flavorings such as vanilla. It is available in bar form as well as chips and pieces.

• **Sweet cooking.** This chocolate must contain 15 percent chocolate liquor, and it almost always has a higher sugar content than semisweet chocolate. It is usually found in 4-ounce bars.

• **Unsweetened cocoa powder.** This is powdered chocolate that has had a portion of the cocoa butter removed. Cocoa keeps indefinitely in a cool place.

• **Dutch process cocoa powder.** This type of cocoa powder is formulated with reduced acidity and gives foods a more mellow flavor. However, it also burns at a lower temperature than more common cocoa.

Like fine wine, dark chocolate actually improves with age. Store it tightly wrapped in a cool place. Even if the chocolate has developed a gray "bloom" from being stored at too high a temperature, it is still fine to use for cooking.

Handle with Care

Except when you're eating chocolate out of your hand or folding chips into cookie dough, chocolate needs a bit of special handling. Use these tips when dealing with the common tasks associated with chocolate.

Chopping chocolate. Chopping it into fine pieces makes melting easier. You can do this in a food processor fitted with a steel blade. Begin by breaking it with a heavy knife rather than breaking it with your hands. Body heat is sufficiently high enough to soften the chocolate so it will not chop evenly.

Melting chocolate. Most chocolate needs careful melting because it scorches easily. You can melt it in a number of ways:

• Melt chunks in the top of a double boiler placed over barely simmering water.

Melting chocolate with a double boiler helps prevent scorching.

• Melt chopped chocolate in a microwave-safe bowl, and microwave on Medium (50 percent power) for 30 seconds. Stir, and repeat as necessary.
• Preheat the oven to 250°F. Place the chopped chocolate in the oven and then turn off the heat immediately. Stir after 3 minutes, and return to the warm oven if necessary.

With all these methods, melt the chocolate until it is just about smooth; the heat in the chocolate will complete the process.

An easy way to dress up bar cookies is by drizzling the pan with dark chocolate or white chocolate before cutting the cookies into pieces. Once the chocolate is melted, dip a spoon into it and then wave the spoon over the cookie pan. An alternate method is to place the melted chocolate in a heavy resealable plastic bag and cut off the tip of one corner.

Baking Basics

These are general pointers on procedures to be used for all genres of baked goods:

• **Measure accurately.** Measure dry ingredients in dry measuring cups, which are plastic or metal and come in sizes of ¼, ⅓, ½, and 1 cup. Spoon dry ingredients from the container or canister into the measuring cup, and then sweep the top with a straight edge such as the back of a knife or a spatula to measure it properly. Do not dip the cup into the canister or tap it on the counter to produce a level surface. These methods pack down the dry ingredients and can increase the actual volume by up to 10 percent. Tablespoons and teaspoons should also be leveled; a rounded ½ teaspoon can really measure almost 1 teaspoon. If the box or can does not have a straight edge built in, level the excess in the spoon back into the container with the back of a knife blade. Measure liquids in liquid measures, which come in different sizes but are transparent glass or plastic and have lines on the sides. To accurately measure liquids, place the measuring cup on a flat counter and bend down to read the marked level.

Dry measuring cups should be used for all dry ingredients.

• **Create consistent temperature.** All ingredients should be at room temperature unless otherwise indicated. Having all ingredients at the same temperature makes it easier to combine them into a smooth, homogeneous mixture. Adding cold liquid to a dough or batter can cause the batter to lose its unified structure by making the fat rigid.

• **Preheat the oven.** Some ovens can take up to 25 minutes to reach a high temperature such as 450°F. The minimum heating time should be 15 minutes.

• **Plan ahead.** Read the recipe thoroughly, and assemble all your ingredients. This means that you have accounted for all ingredients required for a recipe in advance, so you don't get to a step and realize you must improvise. Assembling in advance also lessens the risk of over-mixing dough or batters as the mixer drones on while you search for a specific spice or bag of chips.

Cookie-Specific Tips

Cookies are the easiest of all baked goods to make. That's why every young child begins with making cookies and not sculpting swans from spun sugar. But there are some simple rules to follow:

• Cool your cookie sheets by running the back under cold water between batches. Placing dough on a warm cookie sheet makes the cookies flatten.

• The last few cookies from a batch never seem to have as many "goodies," like chips or nuts as the first few cookies. Reserve some and mix them into the dough after about half of it has been scooped out for cookies. This way, the last of the cookies will have as much good stuff as the first batch.

• Take note of how far apart the mounds of cookie dough for drop cookies should be placed on the baking sheet. Some cookies spread far more than others.

• Rotate the cookie sheets midway through the baking time if using two sheets. Even if baking with a convection fan, cookies on an upper rack brown more quickly than those on a lower rack.

• Always allow cookies to cool for 2 minutes or as instructed in the individual recipe on the baking sheets before transferring them to cooling racks. Until they set up they are very fragile and can easily break apart on the spatula.

Most drop cookie dough can be frozen for up to three months, so you can get a head start on holiday baking or just have cookies around to turn any day into a holiday. Form the dough into balls and arrange them on a cookie sheet lined with parchment or waxed paper. Place the cookie sheet in the freezer. When the balls of dough are frozen, place them in a zipper-lock plastic bag or small airtight container. When you want to make cookies, remove as many balls as you like and bake as directed, increasing the cooking time by a minute or two.

Important Equipment

There is very little specialized equipment need for baking cookies—vegan or otherwise. Here is a list of the machines and gadgets I used regularly while developing the recipes for this book:

• **Microplane grater.** These resemble a flat kitchen spatula but with tiny holes in it. They're fabulous for grating citrus zest and fibrous foods such as ginger, and you can also use them for garlic cloves for other recipes.

• **Food processor.** There is a dedicated corner of my dishwasher given over to workhorse of the kitchen. From chopping nuts and dried fruits to making the dough itself, owning a good food processor is like having a sous chef in the kitchen.

• **Wire cooling racks.** These are essential and there's really no substitute for them. The type of rack on top of a broiler pan is too solid, and there's nothing that makes

A microplane grater is excellent for grating nutmeg.

An offset spatula makes it easy to transfer cookies.

A standard mixer is useful for all baking, including cookies.

crispy cookies soggy faster than placing them on an impervious surface.

• **A powerful mixer.** Some of these cookie doughs are very thick, and a standard mixer that sits on the counter is really a help to make them. While hand-held mixers are fine for small tasks, the stand mixer is best for baking. The paddle makes the thickest substance look easy to blend.

• **Offset spatulas.** These are the type of spatula with the handle raised up from the level of the blade so that transferring cookies from the baking sheets to the cooling racks is comfortable.

Devising a Cookie "Game Plan"

Around the holidays, kitchen efficiency becomes even more important because there's so much cooking to do, in addition to all the other activities that surround the approach of Christmas. If you have only a few hours to spend in the kitchen you want to make sure your cookie production is high.

Start by making a pan of bar cookies; they are quick to assemble but they take the longest time to bake. Once they are in the oven, it's time to make the doughs for rolled cookies that need chilling before they can be baked.

The third type of cookie to make is a batch of drop cookies. The bars are out of the oven, and these cookies don't need chilling time, so they can bake while you roll and cut out the chilled doughs.

Almost all cookies in this book are baked at 350°F, so there's no need for the oven to ever be empty. If you choose a recipe that is baked at 375°F, make those after the other batches.

The Delight of Decorating

Cookies painted with icing or decorated with candies are almost the definition of Christmas cookies. Of course, there are vegan variations on all the traditional methods.

Using Candies and Confections

The collection of colored and flavored sweets that can be affixed to cookies is almost endless. Some of them should be applied before the cookies are baked, and others need to be "glued" on with Royal Icing once cooled.

As a general rule, any candy that can melt, like hard candies, miniature marshmallows, or jellybeans, should be applied after cooking, and any candy that is basically an ingredient, such as the coarse colored sugars found

Vegan shoppers will find a wide range of cookie decorating options.

Candies and frosting should only be applied after cookies are totally cool.

around the holidays, gold or silver dragées, nuts, or candied fruit, should be used before baking. Ingredients such as raisins can be used either way. If they are the "eyes" of gingerbread people or snowmen, it's probably best to place them before baking, but if they're ornaments on a wreath, it's best to add them after the cookie has been frosted.

A way to use colored sugars after cookies are baked is to create patterns with stencils. Spread either Royal Icing or Confectioners' Sugar Glaze on the cooled cookie, and then place a stencil made from parchment paper over it. Sprinkle sugars or jimmies through the hole in the stencil.

Royal Icing

Traditional Royal Icing is made with egg whites. After much experimentation, I developed a vegan formulation that gains the same sheen and density once set.

Yield: 2 cups

Active time: 5 minutes

Start to finish: 5 minutes

¼ cup egg replacement powder, such as Ener-G

¼ teaspoon cream of tartar

4 cups (1 pound) confectioners' sugar

Food coloring (optional)

1. Combine egg replacement powder and ⅓ cup cold water in a mixing bowl. Beat at medium speed with an electric mixer until thick and frothy. Add cream of tartar and beat for 1 minute. Slowly add sugar, and beat for 2 minutes.

2. If tinting icing, transfer it to small cups and add food coloring, a few drops at a time, until desired consistency is reached. Stir well before adding additional coloring.

Note: The icing can be kept at room temperature in an airtight container for up to 2 days. Beat it again lightly to emulsify before using.

Variations:
* *Substitute peppermint oil, almond extract, lemon oil, or orange oil for the vanilla.*

How to Use
Royal Icing of this consistency is perfect to pipe decorations onto cooled cookies, and you can also use it as the "glue" to affix candies. If you want to paint the cookies with frosting, thin the icing with milk in 1-teaspoon amounts until the proper consistency is reached.

"Buttercream" Icing

This icing is richer than Royal Icing, and it is also not bright white because it's made with margarine. It does harden somewhat, but not into a true glaze.

Yield: 2½ cups

Active time: 5 minutes

Start to finish: 5 minutes

½ cup (8 tablespoons) soy margarine, softened

4 cups (1 pound) confectioners' sugar

3 tablespoons plain soy milk or almond milk

½ teaspoon pure vanilla extract

Food coloring (optional)

1. Combine margarine, sugar, milk, and vanilla in a large mixing bowl. Beat at low speed with an electric mixer to blend. Increase the speed to high, and beat for 2 minutes, or until light and fluffy.

2. If tinting icing, transfer it to small cups and add food coloring, a few drops at a time, until desired consistency is reached. Stir well before adding additional coloring.

Note: The icing can be kept refrigerated in an airtight container for up to 5 days. Bring it to room temperature before using.

Variation:
* *Substitute almond extract, lemon oil, or orange oil for the vanilla.*

How to Use:
Buttercream is a wonderful icing to use to make rosettes or other complex decorations with a pastry bag; add additional confectioners' sugar in 1-tablespoon increments if not stiff enough.

Confectioners' Sugar Glaze

This is the easiest and most basic way to cover cooled cookies, and it hardens really well in less than an hour.

Yield: 1½ cups

Active time: 5 minutes

Start to finish: 5 minutes

4 cups (1 pound) confectioners' sugar

4 to 5 tablespoons water

½ teaspoon clear vanilla extract

Food coloring (optional)

1. Combine confectioners' sugar, 4 tablespoons water, and vanilla in a mixing bowl. Stir until smooth, adding additional water if too thick.

2. If tinting glaze, transfer it to small cups and add food coloring, a few drops at a time, until desired consistency is reached. Stir well before adding additional coloring.

Note: The glaze can be kept at room temperature in an airtight container, with a sheet of plastic wrap pressed directly into the surface, for up 6 hours. Beat it again lightly to emulsify before using.

Variations:
* *Substitute orange juice for the water and orange extract for the vanilla.*
* *Substitute peppermint oil or almond extract for the vanilla.*

How to Use:
This glaze is not strong enough to hold large candies, but it can be used as "glue" for small items like jimmies. One way to use it is to spread the white glaze on cooled cookies and allow it to dry hard. Then mix 1 teaspoon of water into ¼ cup of the glaze, and tint it with food coloring. Crumple up a sheet of waxed paper and dip it into the tinted glaze; then dab the cookies and you'll have a marbled effect.

Chocolate Glaze

Yield: 1 cup

Active time: 10 minutes

Start to finish: 10 minutes

2 cups confectioners' sugar

½ cup unsweetened cocoa powder

½ teaspoon pure vanilla extract

¼ cup plain soy milk or almond milk

1. Sift confectioners' sugar and cocoa into a mixing bowl.

2. Add vanilla and all but 1 tablespoon soy milk, and whisk well until smooth. Add remaining soy milk if too thick to use as a glaze.

Note: The icing can be kept refrigerated in an airtight container for up to 5 days. Bring it to room temperature before using.

Variations:
* *Substitute almond extract, peppermint extract, or orange oil for the vanilla.*
* *For mocha frosting, bring the soy milk to a boil and dissolve 1 tablespoon instant espresso powder in it.*

How to Use:
Spread the glaze on top of cooled cookies, or dip one half of a cookie into the chocolate glaze for a two-tone effect. If desired, once the chocolate glaze hardens you can dip the other half of the cookie into Confectioners' Sugar Glaze (page 25).

CHAPTER 2:

Rolled and Formed Cookies

T he recipes in this chapter are for the sorts of the cookies that come to mind right away when you hear "Christmas cookies." Here you'll find flat cookies cut into shapes from trees to angels that are decorated with colored icing and perhaps some candies too. Almost as popular are gingerbread people with tiny smiling faces and buttons down their "jackets." You'll be happy to know that these perennial favorites are easily made using vegan ingredients too.

While these cookies take some time to master, they're not difficult, and once you've made them a few times the whole process of rolling dough will come naturally. Here's a trick I learned from a professional baker that makes keeping the cookies looking good easier. Once the dough is rolled and you've used a cutter to create your shape, it's easier to remove the excess dough rather than trying to move the delicate cookies to the baking sheets. This process is similar to what artists term "relief sculpture." What you are doing is pulling out what is not needed to leave what you want. If you rolled and cut the cookies on a sheet of waxed paper, all you have to do is invert it onto the cookie sheet.

After cut cookies are placed on baking sheets there are always some scraps remaining. Gather these up and chill them if they're too soft to roll again immediately. But only roll any given piece of dough twice, otherwise it becomes tough both from the addition of too much flour and from working the dough too often.

In addition to cookies made with rolled dough, this chapter also contains other traditional forms such as shortbreads and biscotti that are formed by hand.

An Alternative Approach

Any of the rolled cookies can also be baked from chilled logs of dough. There's this whole category called "refrigerator cookies" that fit this bill. You form the dough into a log, and you make the log even by rolling it gently on the counter in the waxed paper. Then you refrigerate the log until it's really firm. Rather than any sort of laborious rolling, you cut off slices from the log and bake them. Some recipes are written for this method, but most can be adapted to it.

If you want to make rolled cookies pretty, decorate them with colored sugar or candies before you bake them, or decorate them with icing after they're cooled.

You can actually hang refrigerator cookies on a small tree as edible ornaments. Before baking them create a small hole at the top with the tip of a paring knife, and make sure the holes have not closed up when the cookies come out of the oven. Loop ribbon through the hole after the cookies cool.

Gingerbread People

Friendly smiling faces on gingerbread cookies have been thrilling generations of children and adults alike. The spicing in this version is accentuated by the addition of freshly ground black pepper, a trick you can use with any baked treat flavored with ginger.

Yield: 3 dozen (3-inch) cookies

Active time: 25 minutes

Start to finish: 1¾ hours, including 1 hour to chill dough

¾ cup (12 tablespoons) soy margarine, softened

½ cup firmly packed light brown sugar

⅔ cup unsulfured molasses

¼ cup silken tofu

1 teaspoon baking soda

1½ teaspoons ground ginger

1 teaspoon apple pie spice

½ teaspoon salt

½ teaspoon pure vanilla extract

¼ teaspoon freshly ground black pepper

2 cups all-purpose flour

1 cup whole-wheat pastry flour

Royal Icing (page 21) or Confectioners' Sugar Glaze (page 25)

Small candies (optional)

1. Combine margarine and sugar in a mixing bowl, and beat at low speed with an electric mixer to blend. Increase the speed to high, and beat for 3 to 4 minutes, or until light and fluffy. Beat in molasses, tofu, baking soda, ginger, apple pie spice, salt, vanilla, and pepper, and beat for 1 minute. Slowly add all-purpose and whole-wheat flours to margarine mixture, and beat until stiff dough forms.

2. Divide dough in half, and wrap each half in plastic wrap. Press dough into a pancake. Refrigerate dough for 1 hour, or until firm, or up to 2 days.

3. Preheat the oven to 350°F. Line two baking sheets with parchment paper or silicone baking mats.

4. Lightly dust a sheet of waxed paper and a rolling pin with flour. Roll dough to a thickness of ¼ inch. Dip cookie cutters in flour, and cut out cookies. Remove excess dough, and transfer cookies to the baking sheets. Re-roll excess dough, chilling it for 15 minutes, if necessary.

5. Bake cookies for 10 to 12 minutes, or until firm. Cool cookies for 2 minutes on the baking sheets, and then transfer cookies to racks to cool completely. Decorate cooled cookies with Confectioners' Sugar Glaze (page 25), and candies, if using.

Note: Keep cookies in an airtight container, layered between sheets of waxed paper or parchment, at room temperature for up to 5 days. Cookies can also be frozen for up to 2 months. Do not freeze cookies if decorated.

Variation:
✳ *Add ½ cup chopped raisins to the dough, and bake the cookies as drop cookies for 13 to 15 minutes. No chilling is necessary for drop cookies.*

Apple pie spice is a combination of fragrant spices that are pre-blended, so you don't have to purchase all of them individually. You can make your own by combining ½ teaspoon cinnamon, ¼ teaspoon nutmeg, ⅛ teaspoon allspice, ⅛ teaspoon ground cardamom, and ¼ teaspoon ground cloves. Or, in a pinch, substitute cinnamon as the primary base, with a dash of any of the other spices you might have on hand.

Christmas Sugar Cookies

These are the cookies that bring out the Pastry Picasso in all of us. They are edible canvases to decorate, and they are the epitome of "Christmas cookie." This vegan version is easy to make too.

Yield: 2 to 3 dozen, depending on the size of the cutters

Active time: 30 minutes

Start to finish: 1¾ hours, including 1 hour to chill dough

1½ teaspoons egg replacement powder, such as Ener-G

¾ cup (12 tablespoons) soy margarine, softened

¾ cup granulated sugar

1 teaspoon pure vanilla extract

½ teaspoon salt

2½ cups all-purpose flour

Royal Icing (page 21) or Confectioners' Sugar Glaze (page 25), optional

Assorted small candies, optional

1. Mix egg replacement powder with 2 tablespoons cold water, and set aside. Combine margarine and sugar in a mixing bowl, and beat at low speed with an electric mixer to blend. Increase the speed to high, and beat for 3 to 4 minutes, or until light and fluffy. Beat in egg replacement mixture, vanilla, and salt, and beat for 1 minute. Slowly add flour to margarine mixture, and beat until stiff dough forms.

2. Divide dough in half, and wrap each half in plastic wrap. Press dough into a pancake. Refrigerate dough for 1 hour, or until firm, or up to 2 days.

3. Preheat the oven to 350°F. Line two baking sheets with parchment paper or silicone baking mats.

4. Lightly dust a sheet of waxed paper and a rolling pin with flour. Roll dough to a thickness of ¼ inch. Dip cookie cutters in flour, and cut out cookies. Remove excess dough, and transfer cookies to the baking sheets. Re-roll excess dough, chilling it for 15 minutes, if necessary.

5. Bake cookies for 10 to 12 minutes, or until edges are brown. Cool cookies for 2 minutes on the baking sheets, and then transfer cookies to racks to cool completely. Decorate cooled cookies with Royal Icing (page 21) or Confectioners' Sugar Glaze (page 25), and candies, if desired.

Note: Keep cookies in an airtight container, layered between sheets of waxed paper or parchment, at room temperature for up to 5 days. Cookies can also be frozen for up to 2 months. Do not freeze cookies if decorated.

Variations:
* *Substitute lemon oil for the vanilla extract, and add 2 teaspoon grated lemon zest to the dough.*
* *Beat the egg replacement mixture with ¼ teaspoon food coloring before adding it to the dough.*
* *Add 1½ teaspoons ground cardamom and 1 tablespoon grated orange zest to the dough.*

Don't have a rolling pin? Cover a glass wine bottle or any sort of round bottle with aluminum foil. Voilà! You've got a rolling pin!

Stained Glass Cookies

These almond-flavored sugar cookies should really be displayed in front of a window to enjoy their visual qualities. Colored hard candies melt into holes made in the dough before baking and become delicious translucent decorations.

Yield: 3 to 4 dozen, depending on the size of the cutters

Active time: 30 minutes

Start to finish: 2 hours, including 1 hour to chill dough

1½ teaspoons egg replacement powder, such as Ener-G

1 cup (16 tablespoons) soy margarine, softened

¾ cup granulated sugar

½ cup firmly packed light brown sugar

½ teaspoon pure almond extract

½ teaspoon salt

3¼ cups all-purpose flour

1 (7-ounce) package brightly colored hard candy, such as sour balls

1. Mix egg replacement powder with 2 tablespoons cold water, and set aside. Combine margarine, granulated sugar, and brown sugar in a mixing bowl, and beat at low speed with an electric mixer to combine. Increase the speed to high, and beat for 3 to 4 minutes, or until light and fluffy. Beat in egg replacement mixture, almond extract, and salt, and beat for 1 minute. Slowly add flour to margarine mixture, and beat until stiff dough forms.

2. Divide dough in half, and wrap each half in plastic wrap. Press dough into a pancake. Refrigerate dough for 1 hour, or until firm, or up to 2 days.

3. While dough chills, divide candies into groupings by color in separate heavy resealable plastic bags. Pound candies with the bottom of a small saucepan until crushed.

4. Preheat the oven to 350°F. Line two baking sheets with parchment paper or silicone baking mats.

5. Lightly dust a sheet of waxed paper and a rolling pin with flour. Roll dough to a thickness of ¼ inch. Dip cookie cutters in flour, and cut out cookies. Remove excess dough, and transfer cookies to the baking sheets. Use smaller cutters to create designs inside of larger cookies. Re-roll excess dough, chilling it for 15 minutes, if necessary. Fill holes in cookies with crushed candy.

6. Bake cookies for 10 to 12 minutes, or until edges are brown. Cool cookies for 5 minutes on the baking sheets, and then transfer cookies to racks to cool completely.

Note: Keep cookies in an airtight container, layered between sheets of waxed paper or parchment, at room temperature for up to 5 days.

Variation:
✳ *Substitute orange oil for the almond extract, and add 1 tablespoon grated orange zest to the dough.*

If you don't have enough cooling racks for cookies you should start them on the rack and then transfer them to sheets of plastic wrap onto which granulated sugar has been sprinkled. The sugar will keep the bottoms from sticking.

Spritz

Spritz are part of the German and Scandinavian Christmas traditions that are now part of the holiday on this continent too. The dough is pressed through a cookie press into fanciful shapes that can be decorated before baking.

Yield: 8 dozen

Active time: 25 minutes

Start to finish: 2 hours, including 1 hour to chill dough

1 tablespoon egg replacement powder, such as Ener-G

1 cup (16 tablespoons) soy margarine, softened

⅔ cup granulated sugar

1 teaspoon pure vanilla extract

¼ teaspoon salt

2½ cups all-purpose flour

Colored coarse sugar crystals

Small candies

Candied cherries

1. Mix egg replacement powder with ¼ cup cold water, and set aside. Combine margarine and sugar in a mixing bowl, and beat at low speed with an electric mixer to blend. Increase the speed to high, and beat for 3 to 4 minutes, or until light and fluffy. Beat in egg replacement mixture, vanilla, and salt, and beat for 1 minute. Slowly add flour to margarine mixture, and beat until soft dough forms.

2. Divide dough in half, and wrap each half in plastic wrap. Press dough into a pancake. Refrigerate dough for 1 hour, or until firm, or up to 2 days.

3. Preheat the oven to 350°F. Line two baking sheets with parchment paper or silicone baking mats.

4. Press dough through a cookie press onto the baking sheets, spacing them 1 inch apart. Decorate cookies with sugar crystals, candies, and candied cherries as desired.

5. Bake cookies for 12 to 15 minutes, or until edges are brown. Cool cookies for 2 minutes on the baking sheets, and then transfer them with a spatula to cooling racks to cool completely.

Note: Keep cookies in an airtight container, layered between sheets of waxed paper or parchment, at room temperature for up to 5 days. Cookies can also be frozen for up to 2 months.

Variations:
✳ *Substitute almond extract for the vanilla extract, and substitute ½ cup almond meal for ½ cup of the flour.*
✳ *Substitute ½ teaspoon orange oil for the vanilla, and add 1 tablespoon grated orange zest to the dough.*
✳ *Substitute ½ teaspoon lemon oil for the vanilla, and add 2 teaspoons grated lemon zest to the dough.*

> **If you don't have a cookie press, you can still make pretty cookies in interesting shapes. Pipe the dough through a pastry bag fitted with a star tip, or pipe the dough through plain tip into circles like a wreath. Then decorate and bake them.**

Linzer Cookies

These cookies are hand-holdable versions of Austria's most famous dessert, the Linzertorte. It is believed to have originated in the city of Linz, and written recipes date back to the early eighteenth century. There's always some sort of nut as part of the pastry, and while in Austria it is filled with black currant preserves, in North America we usually use raspberry.

Yield: 3 dozen

Active time: 35 minutes

Start to finish: 2 hours, including 1 hour to chill dough

1 tablespoon egg replacement powder, such as Ener-G

¾ cup (12 tablespoons) soy margarine, softened

1⅓ cups confectioners' sugar, divided

1½ teaspoons ground cinnamon

1 teaspoon baking powder

½ teaspoon freshly grated nutmeg

½ teaspoon salt

½ teaspoon pure vanilla extract

1¼ cups all-purpose flour

1¼ cups almond meal

½ cup raspberry jam

1. Mix egg replacement powder with ¼ cup cold water, and set aside. Combine margarine and 1 cup sugar in a mixing bowl, and beat at low speed with an electric mixer to blend. Increase the speed to high, and beat for 3 to 4 minutes, or until light and fluffy. Beat in egg replacement mixture, cinnamon, baking powder, nutmeg, salt, and vanilla, and beat for 1 minute. Slowly add flour and almond meal to margarine mixture, and beat until soft dough forms.

2. Divide dough in half, and wrap each half in plastic wrap. Press dough into a pancake. Refrigerate dough for 1 hour, or until firm, or up to 2 days.

3. Preheat oven to 325°F. Line two baking sheets with parchment paper or silicone baking mats.

4. Roll out half of dough on a lightly floured surface to a thickness of ⅛ inch. Using a 2½-inch cutter, cut out rounds. Using a ¾-inch round or star-shaped cutter, cut out center of half of rounds to make rings. Transfer rounds and rings to the prepared baking sheets. Re-roll excess dough, chilling it for 15 minutes, if necessary.

5. Bake cookies for 12 to 15 minutes, or until edges are brown. Cool cookies for 2 minutes on the baking sheets, and then transfer cookies to racks to cool completely.

6. Dust cookies with center hole with remaining confectioners' sugar. Place 1 teaspoon of raspberry jam on solid cookies, and form sandwiches with the two types of cookies.

Note: Keep cookies in an airtight container, layered between sheets of waxed paper or parchment, at room temperature for up to 5 days. Cookies can also be frozen for up to 2 months.

Variations:
✳ *Substitute ground hazelnuts for the almond meal.*
✳ *Substitute blackberry or strawberry jam for the raspberry.*
✳ *Add 1 tablespoon instant espresso powder to the water in addition to the egg replacement powder, and substitute Chocolate Glaze (page 26) for the jam.*

> **Store soft cookies and crisp cookies in different containers to keep the crisp ones crisp, and always store cookies at room temperature.**

Maple Walnut Cookies

Maple has a captivating flavor, and, unlike honey, its vegetal origin is consistent with a vegan diet. In these crispy refrigerator cookies, maple is joined by its New England compatriot, earthy walnuts.

Yield: 5 dozen

Active time: 15 minutes

Start to finish: 2½ hours, including 2 hours to chill dough

1 cup finely chopped walnuts

¾ cup pure maple syrup

½ cup granulated sugar

⅓ cup vegetable oil

¼ cup silken tofu

½ teaspoon pure vanilla extract

1 teaspoon baking powder

¼ teaspoon baking soda

½ teaspoon salt

1½ cups all-purpose flour

1 cup whole-wheat pastry flour

Royal Icing (page 21) or Confectioners' Sugar Glaze (page 25), optional

1. Preheat the oven to 350°F. Place walnuts on a baking sheet, and toast for 5 to 7 minutes, or until browned. Remove walnuts from the oven, and set aside. Turn off the oven. Bring maple syrup to a boil in a small saucepan over medium-high heat. Boil until reduced to ½ cup. Set aside to cool.

2. Combine reduced syrup, sugar, and oil in a mixing bowl, and beat at low speed with an electric mixer to blend. Add tofu, vanilla, baking powder, baking soda, and salt and beat for 1 minute. Slowly add all-purpose and whole-wheat flours to maple mixture, and beat until soft dough forms. Stir in walnuts.

3. Place dough on a sheet of waxed paper, and form it into a log 2½-inches in diameter. Refrigerate dough covered in plastic wrap for 2 hours, or until firm, or up to 2 days.

4. Preheat the oven to 350°F. Line two baking sheets with parchment paper or silicone baking mats.

5. Cut chilled dough into ¼-inch slices using a sharp serrated knife, and arrange them on the baking sheets.

6. Bake cookies for 10 to 12 minutes, or until edges are brown. Cool cookies for 2 minutes on the baking sheets, and then transfer cookies to racks to cool completely. Decorate cookies with Royal Icing or Confectioners' Sugar Glaze, if using.

Note: Keep cookies in an airtight container, layered between sheets of waxed paper or parchment, at room temperature for up to 5 days. Cookies can also be frozen for up to 2 months.

Variation:
✻ *Substitute pecans for the walnuts, and add ½ teaspoon ground ginger to the dough.*

Baking powder does not live forever, and if you haven't used it in a while try this test: Mix 2 teaspoons of baking powder with 1 cup of hot tap water. If there's an immediate reaction of fizzing and foaming, the baking powder can be used. If the reaction is at all delayed or weak, throw the baking powder away and buy a fresh can.

Chocolate Chip Rounds

Regardless of the time of year, everyone loves chocolate chip cookies. These are dressed up as crispy rounds, with the chips on top rather than within.

Yield: 3 dozen cookies

Active time: 15 minutes

Start to finish: 2½ hours, including 2 hours to chill dough

1½ teaspoons egg replacement powder, such as Ener-G

¾ cup (12 tablespoons) soy margarine, softened

½ cup granulated sugar

¾ teaspoon pure vanilla extract

1¾ cups all-purpose flour

1½ cups miniature chocolate chips

1. Mix egg replacement powder with 2 tablespoons cold water, and set aside. Combine margarine, sugar, and vanilla in a mixing bowl, and beat at low speed with an electric mixer to blend. Increase the speed to high, and beat for 3 to 4 minutes, or until light and fluffy. Reduce the speed to medium and add egg replacement mixture. Beat well, reduce the speed to low, and add flour.

2. Place dough on a sheet of waxed paper, and form it into a log 2½-inches in diameter. Refrigerate dough covered in plastic wrap for 2 hours, or until firm, or up to 2 days.

3. Preheat the oven to 350°F. Line two baking sheets with parchment paper or silicone baking mats. Slice logs into ⅓-inch slices, and place them 1 inch apart on the prepared baking sheets. Pat chocolate chips into tops of cookies.

4. Bake cookies for 12 to 15 minutes, or until edges are lightly browned. Cool cookies for 2 minutes on the baking sheets, and then transfer cookies to racks to cool completely.

Note: The cookies can be made up to 5 days in advance and kept at room temperature in an airtight container. Also, the logs can be refrigerated for up to 3 days or frozen for up to 3 months.

Variations:
* *Substitute orange oil for the vanilla extract and add 1 tablespoon grated orange zest to the dough.*
* *Substitute crushed red and white peppermint candies for the chocolate chips.*

> The chocolate chip cookie was developed in 1930 by Ruth Graves Wakefield, owner of the Toll House Inn in Whitman, Massachusetts. The restaurant's popularity was not just due to its home-cooked style meals; her policy was to give diners a whole extra helping of their entrées to take home with them and a serving of her homemade cookies for dessert.

Peppermint Pinwheels

Combining pink dough flavored with peppermint and white dough creates a delicious cookie that looks harder to make than it is. Peppermint is part and parcel of Christmas, and here's another way to enjoy it.

Yield: 2 dozen

Active time: 20 minutes

Start to finish: 3¾ hours, including 3 hours to chill dough

2½ teaspoons egg replacement powder, such as Ener-G

1½ cups all-purpose flour

⅔ cup granulated sugar

½ teaspoon baking soda

¼ teaspoon salt

½ cup (8 tablespoons) soy margarine, chilled and cut into small bits

½ teaspoon peppermint oil or pure peppermint extract

3 to 5 drops red food coloring

Make sure the log is well wrapped in plastic wrap when it's refrigerated the second time. If it's not secure, the dough can dry out and be difficult to cut.

1. Mix egg replacement powder with 3 tablespoons cold water, and set aside. Combine flour, sugar, baking soda, and salt in a food processor fitted with the steel blade. Blend for 5 seconds. Add margarine to the work bowl, and process, using on-and-off pulsing, until mixture resembles coarse meal.

2. Drizzle egg replacement mixture into the work bowl, and pulse about 10 times, or until stiff dough forms.

3. Remove half of dough from the food processor, and set aside. Add peppermint oil and food coloring to the food processor and process until dough is evenly colored. Wrap each dough in plastic wrap. Press dough into a pancake. Refrigerate dough for 1 hour, or until firm, or up to 2 days.

4. Roll out each dough separately into a rectangle approximately ¼-inch thick. Place peppermint dough on top of vanilla dough, and press together around the edges. Using waxed paper or flexible cutting board underneath as a guide, roll dough into a log shape. Wrap in plastic wrap and refrigerate for 2 hours.

5. Preheat the oven to 350°F. Line two baking sheets with parchment paper or silicone baking mats.

6. Cut chilled dough into slices ¼-inch thick with a sharp serrated knife, and arrange them on the baking sheets.

7. Bake cookies for 10 to 12 minutes, or until edges are brown. Cool cookies for 2 minutes on the baking sheets, and then transfer them with a spatula to cooling racks to cool completely.

Note: Keep cookies in an airtight container, layered between sheets of waxed paper or parchment, at room temperature for up to 5 days. Cookies can also be frozen for up to 2 months.

Variations:
✳ *Substitute green food coloring for the red food coloring, and add ½ cup crushed peppermint candies to the vanilla dough.*
✳ *Substitute pure orange oil for the peppermint extract, and color the dough with orange food coloring.*

Piña Colada Sandwich Cookies

Coconut, pineapple, and rum is as delicious a combination in an easy-to-make sandwich cookie as it is in a tropical drink. You can do these cookies without the filling too.

Yield: 4 dozen

Active time: 25 minutes

Start to finish: 3 hours, including 2 hours to chill dough

1 cup sweetened shredded coconut

1¼ cups (20 tablespoons) soy margarine, softened, divided

⅓ cup granulated sugar

1 teaspoon rum extract

2 cups all-purpose flour

½ teaspoon salt

Colored sugar crystals (optional)

1¼ cups confectioners' sugar

2 tablespoons dark rum

3 tablespoons finely chopped dried pineapple

1. Preheat the oven to 325°F. Place coconut on a baking sheet, and toast for 10 to 12 minutes, stirring occasionally, or until flakes are lightly browned. Remove coconut from the oven, and set aside. Turn off the oven.

2. Combine 1 cup margarine, granulated sugar, and rum extract in a mixing bowl, and beat at low speed with an electric mixer to blend. Increase the speed to high, and beat for 3 to 4 minutes, or until light and fluffy. Slowly add flour and salt to the margarine mixture, and beat until soft dough forms. Beat in cooled coconut.

3. Place dough on a sheet of waxed paper, and form it into a log 2½-inches in diameter. Refrigerate dough covered in plastic wrap for 2 hours, or until firm, or up to 2 days.

4. Preheat the oven to 350°F. Line two baking sheets with parchment paper or silicone baking mats.

5. Cut chilled dough into ¼-inch slices using a sharp serrated knife, and arrange them on the baking sheets. Decorate cookies with sugar crystals, if using.

6. Bake cookies for 10 to 12 minutes, or until edges are brown. Cool cookies for 2 minutes on the baking sheets, and then transfer cookies to racks to cool completely.

7. For filling, combine confectioners' sugar, remaining margarine, and rum in a mixing bowl, and beat at low speed with an electric mixer to combine. Increase the speed to high, and beat for 2 to 3 minutes, or until light and fluffy. Stir in pineapple.

8. Place 1 teaspoon of filling on the flat side of half of cookies, and top with the flat side of another cookie. Refrigerate cookies for 15 minutes to firm filling.

Note: Keep unfilled cookies in an airtight container, layered between sheets of waxed paper or parchment, at room temperature for up to 5 days.

Variations:
✻ *Substitute pure vanilla extract for the rum extract, and substitute finely chopped candied orange peel for the dried pineapple.*
✻ *Substitute almond extract for the rum extract, and substitute unsweetened cocoa powder for the dried pineapple.*

Candied Fruit Shortbread Slivers

Candied fruit is such a wonderful ingredient in holiday baking. It's both colorful and flavorful, and it also adds a chewy texture. It's a delicious addition to these spice-scented shortbread cookies.

Yield: 2 dozen

Active time: 15 minutes

Start to finish: 45 minutes

1 cup (16 tablespoons) soy margarine, softened

1½ cups granulated sugar

1 teaspoon pure vanilla extract

½ teaspoon apple pie spice

2 cups all-purpose flour

½ cup cornstarch

½ cup finely chopped candied fruit

Colored sugar crystals

1. Preheat the oven to 350°F, and grease two (10-inch) pie plates.

2. Combine margarine, sugar, and vanilla in a mixing bowl, and beat at low speed with an electric mixer until blended. Increase the speed to high, and beat for 3 to 4 minutes, or until light and fluffy. Reduce the speed to low, and add apple pie spice, flour, and cornstarch. Beat until well blended. Stir in candied fruit.

3. Press dough into the prepared pie plates, extending the sides up ½ inch. Cut dough into 12 thin wedges. Prick surface of dough all over with the tines of a fork. Pat dough with sugar crystals.

4. Bake for 30 minutes, or until dough is lightly browned at the edges. Remove the pans from the oven, and go over cut lines again. Cool completely in the pans on a wire rack, and then remove slivers from the pie plates with a small spatula.

Note: Keep cookies in an airtight container, layered between sheets of waxed paper or parchment, at room temperature for up to 5 days. Cookies can also be frozen for up to 2 months.

Variations:
* *Substitute 1 cup miniature chocolate chips for the candied fruit, and omit the apple pie spice.*
* *Substitute 1 cup slivered almonds, toasted in a 350°F oven for 5 to 7 minutes, or until lightly browned, for the candied fruit, omit the apple pie spice, and substitute pure almond extract for the vanilla extract.*
* *Substitute ½ cup dried cranberries for the candied fruit, omit the apple pie spice, and add 1 tablespoon grated orange zest to the dough.*
* *Substitute ½ cup chopped crystallized ginger for the candied fruit, and substitute ground ginger for the apple pie spice.*

When baking vegan cookies, there are many ways to replace the eggs, depending on their purpose in a non-vegan recipe. Cornstarch is a great substitute in some recipes because it binds ingredients together in the same way that an egg does.

Coffee Ginger Shortbread Slivers

With the sophisticated combination of heady coffee and spicy crystallized ginger in the dough, these cookies will please a crowd of adults.

Yield: 2 dozen

Active time: 15 minutes

Start to finish: 45 minutes

1 tablespoon instant espresso powder

1 cup (16 tablespoons) soy margarine, softened

¾ cup firmly packed light brown sugar

1½ teaspoons ground ginger

½ teaspoon ground cinnamon

¼ teaspoon salt

2 cups all-purpose flour

½ cup whole-wheat pastry flour

½ cup finely chopped crystallized ginger

3 tablespoons granulated sugar

1. Preheat the oven to 350°F, and grease two (10-inch) pie plates. Combine espresso powder with 2 tablespoons boiling water, and stir well. Set aside.

2. Combine margarine and sugar in a mixing bowl, and beat at low speed with an electric mixer until blended. Increase the speed to high, and beat for 3 to 4 minutes, or until light and fluffy. Reduce the speed to low, and add coffee mixture, ginger, cinnamon, salt, and the all-purpose and pastry flours.

3. Press dough into the prepared pie plates, extending the sides up ½ inch. Pat on crystallized ginger and sprinkle with granulated sugar evenly. Cut dough into 12 thin wedges. Prick surface of dough all over with the tines of a fork.

4. Bake for 30 minutes, or until dough is lightly browned at the edges. Remove the pans from the oven, and go over cut lines again. Cool completely in the pans on a wire rack, and then remove slivers from the pie plates with a small spatula.

Note: Keep cookies in an airtight container, layered between sheets of waxed paper or parchment, at room temperature for up to 5 days. Cookies can also be frozen for up to 2 months.

Variations:
* *Omit the coffee mixture and cinnamon, and add 1 tablespoon grated orange zest to the dough.*
* *Add 3 tablespoons unsweetened cocoa powder to the boiling water with the coffee powder, and add 2 tablespoons granulated sugar to the dough.*

> **Crystallized ginger is fresh ginger that is preserved by being candied in sugar syrup. It's then tossed with coarse sugar. It's very expensive in little bottles in the spice aisle, but most whole foods markets sell it in bulk.**

Lemon-Glazed Tea Shortbread Slivers

It's become very chic in the past few years to use tea leaves as an ingredient in addition to brewing them into a beverage. They add a subtle fragrance as well as flavor to these cookies, topped with a lemony glaze.

Yield: 2 dozen

Active time: 15 minutes

Start to finish: 45 minutes

2 tablespoons Earl Grey tea leaves

1½ cups granulated sugar, divided

1 cup (16 tablespoons) soy margarine, softened

½ teaspoon pure vanilla extract

2 cups all-purpose flour

½ cup cornstarch

¼ teaspoon salt

1½ cups confectioners' sugar

1 tablespoon grated lemon zest

3 tablespoons freshly squeezed lemon juice

1. Preheat the oven to 350ºF, and grease two (10-inch) pie plates.

2. Combine tea leaves and ½ cup sugar in a food processor fitted with the steel blade or in a blender. Process until smooth, and transfer mixture to a mixing bowl. Add remaining sugar, margarine, and vanilla, and beat at low speed with an electric mixer until blended. Increase the speed to high, and beat for 3 to 4 minutes, or until light and fluffy. Reduce the speed to low, and add flour, cornstarch, and salt. Beat until well blended.

3. Press dough into the prepared pie plates, extending the sides up ½ inch. Cut dough into 12 thin wedges. Prick surface of dough all over with the tines of a fork.

4. Bake for 30 minutes, or until dough is lightly browned at the edges. Remove the pans from the oven, and go over cut lines again. Cool completely in the pans on a wire rack.

5. Combine confectioners' sugar, lemon zest, and lemon juice in a bowl. Whisk well. Spread glaze over shortbreads, and allow to set for 15 minutes. Remove slivers from the pie plates with a small spatula.

Note: Keep cookies in an airtight container, layered between sheets of waxed paper or parchment, at room temperature for up to 5 days. Cookies can also be frozen for up to 2 months.

Variation:
✳ *Substitute lime juice and lime zest for the lemon juice and lemon zest.*

> **The easiest way to get the most juice out of lemons or limes is to have the fruit at room temperature and roll it around on a counter a few times before cutting it in half. If you need just a few tablespoons of juice, squeeze the juice through the fingers of your other hand. That way you can catch and discard the seeds.**

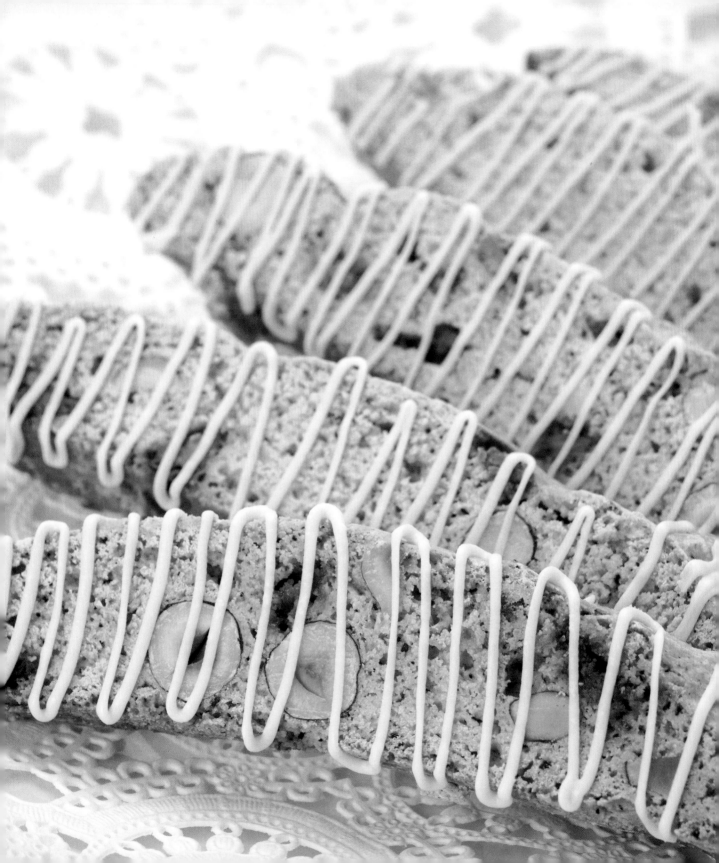

Almond Biscotti

This is a traditional Italian recipe for crispy twice-baked cookies that is popular at all times of year, not just at Christmas. Biscotti also keep very well due to their low moisture content.

Yield: 3 dozen

Active time: 20 minutes

Start to finish: 1¾ hours

1½ cups sliced almonds

2 cups all-purpose flour

½ cup almond meal

½ cup whole-wheat pastry flour

1 cup granulated sugar

2 teaspoons baking powder

¼ teaspoon salt

¾ cup smooth unsweetened applesauce

4 tablespoons soy margarine, melted

1 teaspoon pure almond extract

½ teaspoon pure vanilla extract

1. Preheat the oven to 350°F. Line a baking sheet with parchment paper or a silicone baking mat.

2. Place almonds on a baking sheet, and toast for 5 to 7 minutes, or until lightly browned. Remove almonds from the oven, and set aside.

3. Combine all-purpose flour, almond meal, whole-wheat flour, sugar, baking powder, and salt in a mixing bowl. Whisk well. Add applesauce, margarine, almond extract, and vanilla extract. Beat until stiff dough forms. Fold almonds into dough.

4. Form dough into two logs (3-inches wide) on the prepared baking sheet. Bake until light golden, about 40 minutes. Cool for 30 minutes.

5. Place logs on a cutting board. Cut logs on a diagonal into ½- to ¾-inch-thick slices using a sharp, serrated knife. Arrange biscotti, cut side down, on the baking sheet. Bake for 15 minutes, or until pale golden. Cool cookies for 2 minutes on the baking sheets, and then transfer cookies to racks to cool completely.

Note: Keep cookies in an airtight container, layered between sheets of waxed paper or parchment, at room temperature for up to 2 weeks. Cookies can also be frozen for up to 2 months.

Variations:
* *Substitute chopped pecans, hazelnuts, walnuts, or pistachio nuts for the almonds, and substitute pure vanilla extract for the almond extract.*
* *Add ¼ cup unsweetened cocoa powder and an additional 3 tablespoons sugar to the dough.*

If you want soft biscotti rather than crispy ones, don't bake them a second time. Bake them for 45 minutes, and then let the log cool for 5 minutes before slicing.

Chocolate Peppermint Biscotti

The combination of chocolate and peppermint is a holiday favorite, and in this case the crispy biscotti are dressed up with a bit of icing and some crushed candies to reinforce the minty freshness.

Yield: 3 dozen

Active time: 25 minutes

Start to finish: 2 hours

1½ cups all-purpose flour

¾ cup whole-wheat pastry flour

½ cup unsweetened cocoa powder

1 tablespoon baking powder

¼ teaspoon salt

12 tablespoons soy margarine, softened, divided

1 cup granulated sugar

⅔ cup silken tofu

¾ teaspoon peppermint oil or pure peppermint extract, divided

1 cup confectioners' sugar

½ cup crushed red and white peppermint candies

1. Preheat the oven to 350°F. Line a baking sheet with parchment paper or a silicone baking mat.

2. Combine all-purpose flour, whole-wheat flour, cocoa, baking powder, and salt in a mixing bowl. Whisk well.

3. Combine 8 tablespoons margarine and granulated sugar in another mixing bowl and beat at low speed with an electric mixer to combine. Increase the speed to high, and beat for 3 to 4 minutes, or until light and fluffy. Add tofu and ½ teaspoon peppermint oil, and beat for 1 minute.

4. Slowly add dry ingredients to margarine mixture, and beat until stiff dough forms.

5. Form dough into a log 12-inches long and 3-inches wide on the prepared baking sheet. Bake until crust is hard, about 40 minutes. Cool for 30 minutes.

6. Place log on a cutting board. Cut log on a diagonal into ½ to ¾-inch-thick slices using a sharp, serrated knife. Arrange biscotti, cut side down, on the baking sheet. Bake for 15 minutes, or until crisp. Cool cookies for 2 minutes on the baking sheets, and then transfer cookies to racks to cool completely.

7. For frosting, combine remaining margarine, confectioners' sugar, and remaining peppermint oil in a mixing bowl. Beat at low speed with an electric mixer to combine. Increase the speed to high, and beat for 2 to 3 minutes, or until light and fluffy.

8. Spread frosting on top of thin edge of cookies, and pat peppermint candies on top of frosting.

Note: Keep cookies in an airtight container, layered between sheets of waxed paper or parchment, at room temperature for up to 2 weeks. Cookies can also be frozen for up to 2 months.

Variation:
* *Substitute vanilla extract for the peppermint extract, add 1 tablespoon instant espresso powder to the dough, and substitute miniature chocolate chips for the crushed peppermint candies.*

Orange Candied Fruit Biscotti

The aroma of citrus blends with the succulent candied fruit in this biscotti cookie especially appropriate for the holidays.

Yield: 3 dozen

Active time: 20 minutes

Start to finish: 1¾ hours

2 cups all-purpose flour

1 cup whole-wheat pastry flour

1 cup granulated sugar

2 teaspoons baking powder

¼ teaspoon salt

½ cup smooth unsweetened applesauce

¼ cup orange marmalade

4 tablespoons soy margarine, melted

1 tablespoon grated orange zest

½ teaspoon pure vanilla extract

1 cup chopped candied fruit

1. Preheat the oven to 350°F. Line a baking sheet with parchment paper or a silicone baking mat.

2. Combine all-purpose flour, whole-wheat flour, sugar, baking powder, and salt in a mixing bowl. Whisk well. Add applesauce, marmalade, margarine, orange zest, and vanilla. Beat until stiff dough forms. Fold candied fruit into dough.

3. Form dough into two logs (3 inches wide) on the prepared baking sheet. Bake until light golden, about 40 minutes. Cool for 30 minutes.

4. Place logs on a cutting board. Cut logs on a diagonal into ½- to ¾-inch-thick slices using a sharp, serrated knife. Arrange biscotti, cut side down, on the baking sheet. Bake for 15 minutes, or until pale golden. Cool cookies for 2 minutes on the baking sheets, and then transfer cookies to racks to cool completely.

Note: Keep cookies in an airtight container, layered between sheets of waxed paper or parchment, at room temperature for up to 5 days. Cookies can also be frozen for up to 2 months.

Variations:
* *Substitute ¾ cup dried cranberries and ¼ cup chopped pistachio nuts for the candied fruit.*
* *Add 2 tablespoons finely chopped crystallized ginger to the dough.*

Applesauce is frequently used in vegan baking to provide moisture, and it really should be smooth so that it won't change the texture of the finished cookies. If what you have on hand is chunky applesauce, puree it in a blender until it's smooth. If you want just a small amount you can even buy a jar of baby applesauce.

CHAPTER 3:

Dropped and Balled Cookies

Drop cookies are a wonderful category at any time of the year, including the holidays. This category contains such favorites as chocolate chip and oatmeal cookies, as well as peanut butter. For the holidays these homey classics can be dressed up with some of the decorating suggestions given in Chapter 1, and many of the recipes in this chapter contain lots of dried and candied fruits, which makes them more festive as well as nutritious.

In some respects, the word *drop* is inaccurate. Although the dough is softer than for rolled cookies, it really doesn't drop onto the baking sheets without some coaxing. There are two ways to accomplish this task: another spoon or a finger. If using the "two spoon method," spray both spoons with vegetable oil spray first to make it easier to slide the dough off with the other spoon.

The first cousins of this hall of fame are balled cookies. Rather than just depositing the dough on a baking sheet, small portions are rolled into balls. In these cases the cookies emerge from the oven looking far more uniform and elegant and less homey and homemade. Most of the cookies in this chapter can be baked in that manner. If the dough is too soft to roll at first, try chilling it well and it should firm up enough to roll.

While rolled cookies and drop cookies take more time than bar cookies due to portioning the dough, this is a task that has traditionally been given over to children once the dough is made. However, some guidance is needed because the success of drop cookies depends on mounds of a uniform size. The size includes both the diameter of the circle and also its height.

If the cookies are of a uniform size, the difference between chewy cookies and crisp cookies is the baking time. All these recipes have a range given of a few minutes. If you bake them for the minimum amount of time, you'll have a much moister and chewier cookie than if you let them go for the full baking time at which point much of the moisture will have evaporated during the last few moments of baking.

Snowballs

These meltingly tender cookies are sometimes referred to as Mexican Wedding Cookies. They are perennial favorites for the holidays with all generations of cookie lovers.

Yield: 4 dozen

Active time: 15 minutes

Start to finish: 30 minutes

1 cup (16 tablespoons) soy margarine, softened

1¾ cups confectioners' sugar, divided

1 cup cake flour

1 cup self-rising flour

1 cup very finely chopped blanched almonds

½ teaspoon pure vanilla extract, preferably Mexican

1. Preheat the oven to 350°F. Line two baking sheets with parchment paper or silicone baking mats.

2. Combine margarine and 1¼ cups sugar in a mixing bowl, and beat at low speed with an electric mixer to blend. Increase the speed to high, and beat for 3 to 4 minutes, or until light and fluffy. Add cake flour, self-rising flour, almonds, and vanilla to the bowl, and mix briefly until just combined. The dough will be very stiff; add a few drops of hot water, if necessary, to make it pliable.

3. Take scant 1-tablespoon portions of dough, and roll them into balls. Place balls 1 inch apart on the prepared baking sheets, and flatten balls slightly with the bottom of a glass dipped in flour. Bake cookies for 12 to 15 minutes, or until lightly browned.

4. Allow cookies to sit for 2 minutes. Sift remaining ½ cup sugar into a low bowl, and transfer cookies a few at a time to the bowl with a spatula. Coat cookies with sugar, and then transfer cookies to racks to cool completely.

Note: Keep cookies in an airtight container, layered between sheets of waxed paper or parchment, at room temperature for up to 5 days. Cookies can also be frozen for up to 2 months.

Variations:
* *Substitute pecans, toasted in a 350°F oven for 5 to 7 minutes, for the almonds.*
* *Add ⅓ cup unsweetened cocoa powder to the dough.*

Part of the plum family, the almond tree is native to North Africa, West Asia, and the Mediterranean. The English word *almond* is derived from the French *amande*, which in turn is a derivative of the old Latin word for almond, *amygdalus*, literally meaning "tonsil plum."

Crunchy Peanut Butter and Cherry Thumbprints

This is a drop (or ball) cookie recipe that is very much associated with Christmas. The cookie is coated with crunchy nuts, and there's a succulent candied cherry plunked in the middle.

Yield: 3 dozen

Active time: 20 minutes

Start to finish: 45 minutes

1½ teaspoons egg replacement powder, such as Ener-G

¾ cup firmly packed light brown sugar

½ cup (8 tablespoons) soy margarine, softened

1 cup smooth commercial peanut butter (not homemade or natural)

½ teaspoon pure vanilla extract

1 teaspoon baking soda

¼ teaspoon salt

1 cup all-purpose flour

1 cup finely chopped roasted peanuts (not dry-roasted)

18 red or green candied cherries, halved

1. Preheat the oven to 375°F. Line two baking sheets with parchment paper or silicone baking mats.

2. Mix egg replacement powder with 2 tablespoons cold water, and set aside. Combine sugar, margarine, and peanut butter in a mixing bowl, and beat at low speed with an electric mixer to blend. Increase the speed to high, and beat for 3 to 4 minutes, or until light and fluffy. Beat in egg replacement mixture, vanilla, baking soda, and salt and beat for 1 minute. Slowly add flour to margarine mixture, and beat until soft dough forms.

3. Take scant 1-tablespoon portions of dough, and roll them into balls. Roll balls in chopped peanuts. Place balls 1½ inches apart on the baking sheets, and make a shallow depression with your index finger in the center of each ball. Insert 1 cherry half into each depression.

4. Bake cookies for 10 to 12 minutes, or until edges are brown. Cool cookies for 2 minutes on the baking sheets, and then transfer cookies to racks to cool completely.

Note: Keep cookies in an airtight container, layered between sheets of waxed paper or parchment, at room temperature for up to 5 days.

Variations:
* *Substitute commercial almond butter and chopped almonds for the peanut butter and peanuts.*
* *Substitute a few chocolate chips for the cherries, and place them on the cookies prior to baking.*
* *Omit cherries and top cookies with 1 teaspoon raspberry or strawberry jam once cooled.*

George Washington Carver, an educator at the Tuskegee Institute in Alabama, was an avid promoter of peanuts as a replacement for the region's cotton crop, which had been severely damaged by the boll weevil. In his 1916 Research Bulletin called *How to Grow the Peanut and 105 Ways of Preparing It for Human Consumption,* he included three recipes for peanut cookies calling for crushed or chopped peanuts as an ingredient. It was not until the early 1920s that peanut butter is listed as an ingredient in the cookies.

Snickerdoodles

Snickerdoodles, a basic "buttery" cookie rolled in spiced sugar before baking, are a traditional favorite in North America. They are a cookie that's wonderful to get children to help make too.

Yield: 2½ dozen

Active time: 15 minutes

Start to finish: 40 minutes

1 cup (16 tablespoons) soy margarine, softened

1⅔ cups granulated sugar, divided

2 tablespoons soy milk

1 teaspoon pure vanilla extract

1 cup all-purpose flour

⅔ cup whole-wheat pastry flour

2 tablespoons cornstarch

1 teaspoon baking powder

¼ teaspoon salt

1 teaspoon ground cinnamon

¼ teaspoon freshly grated nutmeg

1. Preheat the oven to 350°F. Line two baking sheets with parchment paper or silicone baking mats.

2. Combine margarine, 1¼ cups sugar, soy milk, and vanilla in a mixing bowl, and beat at low speed with an electric mixer to blend. Increase the speed to high, and beat for 3 to 4 minutes, or until light and fluffy. Reduce the speed to low and add all-purpose and whole-wheat flours, cornstarch, baking powder, and salt until just blended in.

3. Combine remaining sugar, cinnamon, and nutmeg in a small bowl. Take scant 1-tablespoon portions of dough, and roll them into balls. Roll balls in sugar mixture. Arrange balls 2 inches apart on the prepared baking sheets.

4. Bake for 12 to 14 minutes, or until lightly brown around the edges. Cool for 2 minutes on the baking sheets, and then transfer cookies to racks to cool completely.

Note: Keep cookies in an airtight container, layered between sheets of waxed paper or parchment, at room temperature for up to 5 days. Cookies can also be frozen for up to 2 months.

Variation:
* *Add ¼ cup finely chopped crystallized ginger to the dough.*

> Snickerdoodles are a traditional American cookie, and it comes from the German baking tradition. The recipes date back to the early nineteenth century, and the only constant is the use of the cinnamon and sugar coating. Some recipes call for cinnamon in the cookie too.

Pineapple Orange Cookies

These easy cookies are like a trip to the tropics. The cookie gets its orange flavor from three sources—zest, aromatic orange oil, and heady Grand Marnier. Then both the flavor and texture becomes more complex with the addition of chopped candied pineapple.

Yield: 3 dozen

Active time: 20 minutes

Start to finish: 35 minutes

1 cup (16 tablespoons) soy margarine, softened

1½ cups confectioners' sugar, divided

2 tablespoons Grand Marnier, triple sec, or other orange-flavored liqueur

2 teaspoons grated orange zest

½ teaspoon pure orange oil

2¼ cups all-purpose flour

¼ teaspoon salt

1 cup finely chopped candied pineapple

1. Preheat the oven to 375°F. Line two baking sheets with parchment paper or silicone baking mats.

2. Combine margarine and ½ cup sugar in a mixing bowl, and beat at low speed with an electric mixer to blend. Increase the speed to high, and beat for 3 to 4 minutes, or until light and fluffy. Beat in Grand Marnier, orange zest, and orange oil, and beat for 1 minute. Slowly add flour and salt to margarine mixture, and beat until soft dough forms. Fold pineapple into dough.

3. Take scant 1-tablespoon portions of dough, and roll them into balls. Place balls 1 inch apart on the prepared baking sheets, and flatten balls slightly with the bottom of glass dipped in flour. Bake cookies for 10 to 12 minutes, or until lightly browned.

4. Allow cookies to sit for 2 minutes. Sift remaining ½ cup sugar into a low bowl, and transfer cookies a few at a time to the bowl with a spatula. Coat cookies with sugar, and then transfer cookies to racks to cool completely.

Note: Keep cookies in an airtight container, layered between sheets of waxed paper or parchment, at room temperature for up to 5 days. Cookies can also be frozen for up to 2 months.

Variation:
* *Substitute candied chopped mixed candied fruit for the pineapple, and substitute rum extract for the vanilla.*

You really don't have to worry about using small amounts of liquor or liqueurs in baking, either for children or for adults who must avoid all alcohol. About 90 percent of the alcohol evaporates during baking; in this small a quantity it will have not any effect on those who eat the cookie.

Dried Fruit Cookies

These are one of the chewiest cookies I make, and the combination of different dried fruits makes them pretty as well as delicious. Tossing the dried fruit with flour keeps it from sticking together too.

Yield: 2 to 3 dozen

Active time: 20 minutes

Start to finish: 35 minutes

½ pound pecans

¼ pound dried apricots, chopped

¼ pound dried figs, stemmed and chopped

¼ pound candied pineapple, chopped

1¼ cups all-purpose flour, divided

½ cup (8 tablespoons) soy margarine, softened

½ cup granulated sugar

½ cup firmly packed light brown sugar

¼ cup silken tofu

1 teaspoon pure vanilla extract

½ teaspoon baking soda

½ teaspoon ground cinnamon

¼ teaspoon salt

1. Preheat the oven to 350°F. Line two baking sheets with parchment paper or silicone baking mats. Place pecans on a baking sheet, and toast for 5 to 7 minutes, or until lightly browned. Remove the pan from the oven, and coarsely chop nuts in a food processor fitted with a steel blade, using on-and-off pulsing, or by hand. Increase the oven temperature to 375ºF.

2. Combine nuts, dried apricots, figs, and candied pineapple in a mixing bowl. Toss with ½ cup four, and mix well so that pieces separate.

3. Combine margarine, granulated sugar, and brown sugar in a large mixing bowl, and beat at low speed with an electric mixer to blend. Increase the speed to high, and beat for 3 to 4 minutes, or until light and fluffy. Add tofu, vanilla, baking soda, cinnamon, and salt, and beat for 1 minute. Reduce the speed to low and add remaining flour until just blended in. Stir in nut and dried fruit mixture.

4. Drop batter by tablespoons onto the baking sheets, spacing them 2 inches apart. Bake for 10 to 12 minutes, or until edges are brown. Cool for 2 minutes on the baking sheets, and then transfer cookies to racks to cool completely.

Note: Keep cookies in an airtight container, layered between sheets of waxed paper or parchment, at room temperature for up to 5 days. Cookies can also be frozen for up to 2 months.

Variation:
✳ *Substitute ground ginger for cinnamon, and add ¼ cup finely chopped crystallized ginger to the dough.*

Cinnamon is the inner bark of a tropical evergreen tree that's harvested during the rainy season and then allowed to dry. At that time it's sold as sticks or ground. What we call cinnamon is cassia cinnamon, and there's also a Ceylon cinnamon that is less pungent.

Bourbon Fruitcake Cups

These festive cookies are laced with heady bourbon and finished with a drizzle of white icing. There's actually more fruit in them than anything else, and even people who say they don't like fruitcakes adore them.

Yield: 3 dozen

Active time: 25 minutes

Start to finish: 3½ hours, including 2 hours to macerate fruit

1 cup raisins

½ cup dried currants

½ cup chopped pitted dates

½ cup candied citrus peel

⅔ cup bourbon, divided

½ cup chopped walnuts

6 tablespoons soy margarine, softened

½ cup firmly packed light brown sugar

¼ cup mashed ripe banana

½ teaspoon pure vanilla extract

½ teaspoon baking powder

½ teaspoon apple pie spice

¼ teaspoon salt

1 cup all-purpose flour

1 cup confectioners' sugar

3 dozen (1-inch) paper baking cups

1. Combine raisins, currants, dates, citrus peel, and ½ cup bourbon in a mixing bowl, and toss well. Allow mixture to sit at room temperature for a minimum of 2 hours, and up to 24 hours, covered with plastic wrap.

2. Preheat the oven to 350°F. Place walnuts on a baking sheet, and toast for 5 to 7 minutes, or until lightly browned. Reduce the oven temperature to 325°F.

3. Combine margarine and brown sugar in a mixing bowl, and beat at low speed with an electric mixer to blend. Increase the speed to high, and beat for 3 to 4 minutes, or until light and fluffy. Beat in banana, vanilla, baking powder, apple pie spice, and salt, and beat for 1 minute. Slowly add flour to margarine mixture, and beat to combine. Fold dried fruit mixture into dough.

4. Drop heaping teaspoons of dough into 1-inch paper baking cups. Arrange filled cups on a baking sheet. Bake for 20 to 24 minutes, or until lightly brown. Transfer cups to a cooling rack, and cool completely.

5. Combine confectioners' sugar and remaining bourbon in a mixing bowl, and beat at low speed with an electric mixer to blend. Drizzle lines of frosting on top of cooled cups.

Note: Keep cookies in an airtight container, layered between sheets of waxed paper or parchment, at room temperature for up to 5 days.

Variation:
* *Substitute rum, Grand Marnier, or Amaretto for the bourbon.*

The reason to toast nuts is to create the best crunchy texture and also to release the aromatic nut oils to achieve the best flavor. Any nuts folded into a batter or dough should be pre-toasted. Nuts placed on top will toast during the baking process.

Pine Nut Currant Cookies

This cookie comes from the Christmas traditions of southern Italy, where pine nuts—called pignoli—are a symbol of good luck. The intensely flavored dried currants add to both the flavor and texture of the cookies.

Yield: 3 dozen

Active time: 15 minutes

Start to finish: 40 minutes

¾ cup pine nuts

1 cup (16 tablespoons) soy margarine, softened

1 cup granulated sugar

1 cup all-purpose flour

¾ cup whole-wheat pastry flour

½ teaspoon pure vanilla extract

¼ teaspoon salt

½ cup dried currants

1. Preheat the oven to 350°F. Line two baking sheets with parchment paper or silicone baking mats.

2. Toast pine nuts in a dry skillet over medium heat for 1 to 1½ minutes, or until just lightly browned. Set aside.

3. Combine margarine and sugar in a mixing bowl, and beat at low speed with an electric mixer to blend. Increase the speed to high, and beat for 3 to 4 minutes, or until light and fluffy. Reduce the speed to low and add all-purpose and whole-wheat flours, vanilla, and salt until just blended in. Stir in dried currants.

4. Take scant 1-tablespoon portions of dough, and roll them into balls. Flatten balls slightly into discs. Press discs into pine nuts. Bake for 15 to 18 minutes, or until lightly brown around the edges. Cool for 2 minutes on the baking sheets, and then transfer cookies to racks to cool completely.

Note: Keep cookies in an airtight container, layered between sheets of waxed paper or parchment, at room temperature for up to 5 days. Cookies can also be frozen for up to 2 months.

Variations:
* *Substitute chopped raisins, chopped figs, or chopped dried apricots for the currants.*
* *Substitute chopped hazelnuts or macadamia nuts for the pine nuts.*

Dried currants are made from the Black Corinth grape, and they're really much closer to raisins than any other fruit. The species of grape was introduced to North America in the mid-nineteenth century. Stories about dried currants date back to ancient history.

Holiday Oatmeal Cookies

The holiday aspect of this healthful cookie made with rolled oats is the inclusion of brightly colored and brightly flavored dried cranberries as well as crispy green pistachio nuts.

Yield: 3 to 4 dozen cookies

Active time: 15 minutes

Start to finish: 30 minutes

1 tablespoon egg replacement powder, such as Ener-G

⅓ cup (6 tablespoons) soy margarine, softened

½ cup granulated sugar

½ cup firmly packed dark brown sugar

1 teaspoon pure vanilla extract

1 teaspoon ground cinnamon

½ teaspoon baking soda

Pinch of salt

1 cup all-purpose flour

1¼ cups quick-cooking or old-fashioned oats (not instant)

1 cup dried cranberries

1 cup chopped pistachio nuts

1. Preheat the oven to 375°F. Line two baking sheets with parchment paper or silicone baking mats.

2. Mix egg replacement powder with ¼ cup cold water, and set aside. Combine margarine, granulated sugar, and brown sugar in a mixing bowl, and beat at low speed with an electric mixer to blend. Increase the speed to high, and beat for 3 to 4 minutes, or until light and fluffy. Add egg replacement mixture, vanilla, cinnamon, baking soda, and salt, and beat for 2 minutes more. Reduce the speed to low and add flour until just blended in. Stir in oats, cranberries, and pistachios.

3. Drop batter by tablespoons onto the baking sheets, spacing them 2 inches apart. Bake for 12 to 15 minutes, or until edges are brown. Cool for 2 minutes on the baking sheets, and then transfer cookies to racks to cool completely.

Note: Keep cookies in an airtight container, layered between sheets of waxed paper or parchment, at room temperature for up to 5 days. Cookies can also be frozen for up to 2 months.

Variations:
* *Substitute chopped dried apricots or raisins for the dried cranberries.*
* *Substitute chopped walnuts or pecans for the pistachios. Toast the walnuts or pecans in a 350ºF oven for 5 to 7 minutes.*

The cranberry, along with the blueberry and Concord grape, is one of North America's three native fruits that are still commercially grown. Native Americans discovered the wild berry's versatility as a food, fabric dye, and healing agent.

Chocolate Chip Oatmeal Cookies

Chocolate chip cookies transform any day into a holiday, and this is a wonderful family-pleasing recipe with lots of high-fiber oats.

Yield: 3 dozen

Active time: 15 minutes

Start to finish: 30 minutes

½ cup (8 tablespoons) soy margarine, softened

½ cup firmly packed light brown sugar

½ cup granulated sugar

½ cup peanut oil

¼ cup mashed ripe banana

1 teaspoon pure vanilla extract

1 cup all-purpose flour

¾ cup whole-wheat pastry flour

1½ teaspoons baking powder

¼ teaspoon salt

1 cup quick oats

1 (12-ounce) package vegan semisweet chocolate chips, or more, to taste

1. Preheat oven to 350ºF. Line two baking sheets with parchment paper or silicone baking mats.

2. Combine margarine, brown sugar, and granulated sugar in a mixing bowl, and beat at low speed with an electric mixer to blend. Increase the speed to high, and beat for 3 to 4 minutes, or until light and fluffy. Add oil, banana, and vanilla, and beat for 1 minute. Reduce the speed to low and add all-purpose and whole-wheat flours, baking powder, and salt until just blended in. Stir in oats and chocolate chips.

3. Drop batter by tablespoons onto the baking sheets, spacing them 2 inches apart. Bake for 12 to 15 minutes, or until edges are brown. Cool for 2 minutes on the baking sheets, and then transfer cookies to racks to cool completely.

Note: Keep cookies in an airtight container, layered between sheets of waxed paper or parchment, at room temperature for up to 5 days. Cookies can also be frozen for up to 2 months.

Variation:
✳ *Substitute raisins or chopped candied or dried fruit for the chocolate chips.*

Many vegan cookie recipes call for small amounts of mashed banana as a substitution for eggs to provide moisture. Go ahead and mash up a whole banana, or even a few, and then freeze the mashed banana in ¼-cup portions. You'll be ready for baking at any time.

Coconut, Oatmeal, and Macadamia Nut Cookies

These cookies transport you to the sunny beaches of Hawaii with the irresistible taste of crunchy macadamia nuts and the chewy texture of coconut.

Yield: 3 dozen

Active time: 20 minutes

Start to finish: 1 hour, including 30 minutes to rest dough

⅔ cup coconut oil or vegetable oil

¾ cup firmly packed light brown sugar

¼ cup silken tofu

½ teaspoon pure vanilla extract

1 teaspoon baking powder

½ teaspoon ground cinnamon

¼ teaspoon baking soda

¼ teaspoon salt (omit if using salted macadamia nuts)

1½ cups all-purpose flour

1 cup shredded sweetened coconut

¾ cup rolled oats

1¼ cups chopped unsalted roasted macadamia nuts

1. Combine oil and sugar in a saucepan over medium heat. Cook over low heat until sugar mixture is bubbly. Remove the pan from the heat.

2. Whisk in tofu, vanilla, baking powder, cinnamon, baking soda, and salt. Stir in flour, and then fold in coconut, oats, and macadamia nuts. Set aside for 30 minutes, or until mixture reaches room temperature and thickens.

3. Preheat the oven to 400°F. Line two baking sheets with parchment paper or silicone baking mats.

4. Drop batter by tablespoons onto the baking sheets, spacing them 2 inches apart. Bake for 10 to 12 minutes, or until edges are brown. Cool for 2 minutes on the baking sheets, and then transfer cookies to racks to cool completely.

Note: Keep cookies in an airtight container, layered between sheets of waxed paper or parchment, at room temperature for up to 5 days. Cookies can also be frozen for up to 2 months.

Variation:
✽ *Substitute almonds for the macadamia nuts, and substitute almond extract for the vanilla extract.*

> **While we consider macadamia nuts to be Hawaiian, they are native to Australia, which remains the largest commercial producer of these tropical nuts. The group of nine species is named after John Macadam, the botanist who first noticed them in the nineteenth century.**

Granola Cookies

These cookies taste as if they're complicated to make because they contain myriad ingredients. But one of those ingredients is trail mix. They can be a healthful alternative to other more decadent Christmas treats too.

Yield: 4 dozen

Active time: 15 minutes

Start to finish: 30 minutes

1 tablespoon egg replacement powder, such as Ener-G

1 cup (16 tablespoons) soy margarine, softened

1 cup firmly packed light brown sugar

¾ cup granulated sugar

1 teaspoon pure vanilla extract

¾ cup all-purpose flour

½ cup whole wheat flour

1 teaspoon baking soda

½ teaspoon baking powder

½ teaspoon ground cinnamon

¼ teaspoon salt

2 cups old-fashioned oats

½ cup unsweetened flaked coconut

2 cups trail mix, coarsely chopped

1. Preheat the oven to 350°F, and grease two baking sheets or line them with silicone baking mats.

2. Mix egg replacement powder with ¼ cup cold water, and set aside. Combine margarine, brown sugar, and granulated sugar in a mixing bowl, and beat at low speed with an electric mixer to blend. Increase the speed to high, and beat for 3 to 4 minutes, or until light and fluffy. Beat in egg replacement mixture and vanilla. Beat in all-purpose flour, whole-wheat flour, baking soda, baking powder, cinnamon, and salt at low speed. Stir in oats, coconut, and trail mix by hand.

3. Drop dough by tablespoons onto prepared baking sheets, 1½ inches apart. Bake cookies for 12 to 15 minutes, or until browned. Allow cookies to cool for 3 minutes on baking sheets, and then transfer cookies to racks to cool completely.

Note: Keep cookies in an airtight container, layered between sheets of waxed paper or parchment, at room temperature for up to 5 days. Cookies can also be frozen for up to 2 months.

Variation:
✱ *Substitute ground ginger for the cinnamon and substitute granola cereal for the trail mix.*

It's now fairly easy to find unsweetened coconut in the bulk food sections of whole food markets and the natural food sections of supermarkets, where most vegan ingredients are shelved. But if you end up with sweetened coconut, reduce the granulated sugar by 2 tablespoons for each ½ cup of coconut.

Banana Nut Ginger Cookies

The combination of cashews and almonds is wonderful in this cookie that uses sweet ripe banana both for its flavor and moisture. The crystallized ginger in the dough adds sparkle to the flavor too.

Yield: 2½ dozen

Active time: 15 minutes

Start to finish: 30 minutes

½ cup chopped unsalted cashews

½ cup chopped blanched almonds

1 large ripe banana

1 cup all-purpose flour

½ cup vegetable oil

½ teaspoon baking soda

½ teaspoon ground ginger

¼ teaspoon salt

1½ cups old-fashioned oats

¼ cup finely chopped crystallized ginger

1. Preheat the oven to 350°F. Line two baking sheets with parchment paper or silicone baking mats. Place cashews and almonds on a baking sheet, and toast for 5 to 7 minutes, or until lightly browned.

2. Place banana in a mixing bowl, and mash until smooth. Stir in flour, oil, baking soda, ginger, and salt. Beat well. Stir in oats, ginger, and toasted nuts. Mix well using a sturdy spoon.

3. Drop batter by tablespoons onto the baking sheets, spacing them 2 inches apart. Bake for 10 to 12 minutes, or until edges are brown. Cool for 2 minutes on the baking sheets, and then transfer cookies to racks to cool completely.

Note: Keep cookies in an airtight container, layered between sheets of waxed paper or parchment, at room temperature for up to 5 days. Cookies can also be frozen for up to 2 months.

Variations:
* *Substitute pecans for the cashews and almonds, omit the ginger, and add 1 teaspoon ground cinnamon to the dough.*
* *Substitute walnuts and toasted walnut oil or hazelnuts and toasted hazelnut oil for the cashews and almonds and vegetable oil; omit the ginger.*

> Just because bananas are put out in big bunches doesn't mean you have to buy them that way. If you only go grocery shopping every four or five days, what makes the most sense is to buy a few ripe bananas, and then a few that need a few days to ripen. I sometimes have a whole bag of single bananas in the checkout line.

Ginger Maple Cookies

These cookies are a lot easier to make than gingerbread people, and there's a surprise in the maple flavor complementing the ginger.

Yield: 3 dozen

Active time: 20 minutes

Start to finish: 45 minutes

¾ cup (12 tablespoons) soy margarine, softened

1 cup maple sugar

¼ cup silken tofu

¼ cup pure maple syrup

½ cup finely chopped crystallized ginger

2 teaspoons baking soda

1 teaspoon ground ginger

¼ teaspoon salt

2½ cups all purpose flour

½ cup granulated sugar

1. Preheat the oven to 350°F. Line two baking sheets with parchment paper or silicone baking mats.

2. Combine margarine and maple sugar in a mixing bowl, and beat at low speed with an electric mixer to blend. Increase the speed to high, and beat for 3 to 4 minutes, or until light and fluffy. Beat in tofu, maple syrup, crystallized ginger, baking soda, ground ginger, and salt and beat for 1 minute. Slowly add flour to margarine mixture, and beat until soft dough forms.

3. Take scant 1-tablespoon portions of dough, and roll them into balls. Roll balls in granulated sugar. Place balls 1½ inches apart on the baking sheets.

4. Bake cookies for 12 to 15 minutes, or until top surface is cracked. Cool cookies for 2 minutes on the baking sheets, and then transfer cookies to racks to cool completely.

Note: Keep cookies in an airtight container, layered between sheets of waxed paper or parchment, at room temperature for up to 5 days. Cookies can also be frozen for up to 2 months.

Variation:
✱ *Substitute firmly packed light brown sugar for maple sugar, and substitute light molasses for maple syrup.*

> **Early New England settlers sweetened foods with maple syrup because white sugar had to be imported and was, therefore, expensive. Tapping the sugar maple trees native to North America and creating syrup from the sap is another skill the Native Americans taught the settlers.**

Mocha Crackles

There is something magical that happens when chocolate and coffee are joined to create mocha. These deeply colored cookies are coated with confectioners' sugar after baking, which makes them more of a holiday treat.

Yield: 3 dozen

Active time: 20 minutes

Start to finish: 45 minutes

2 tablespoons instant coffee

2 tablespoons boiling water

½ cup (8 tablespoons) soy margarine, softened

2 cups confectioners' sugar, divided

¼ cup silken tofu

½ teaspoon pure vanilla extract

¼ cup unsweetened cocoa powder

⅔ cup all-purpose flour

⅔ cup whole-wheat pastry flour

Pinch of salt

1. Preheat the oven to 350°F. Line two baking sheets with parchment paper or silicone baking mats. Combine coffee powder and boiling water in a small bowl, and stir well to dissolve coffee. Set aside to cool.

2. Combine margarine and ½ cup sugar in a mixing bowl, and beat at medium speed with an electric mixer until light and fluffy. Add tofu and vanilla, and beat well. Add cocoa powder and coffee mixture, and beat well, scraping the sides of the bowl as necessary. Reduce the speed to low, and add all-purpose and whole-wheat flours, and salt. Beat until just combined.

3. Form dough into 1-inch balls, and place them 1 inch apart on the prepared baking sheets. Bake for 15 to 18 minutes, or until firm. Sift remaining confectioners' sugar into a low bowl, and add a few cookies at a time, rolling them around in the sugar to coat them well. Transfer cookies to racks to cool completely.

Note: Keep cookies in an airtight container, layered between sheets of waxed paper or parchment, at room temperature for up to 5 days. Cookies can also be frozen for up to 2 months.

Variation:
✳ *For chocolate cookies, omit the instant coffee, increase the cocoa powder to ⅓ cup, and add 2 tablespoons cold water to the dough.*

> The best way to measure flour is by weighing it; that's the way professional pastry chefs do it. The reason is that how you treat the flour can influence the amount you get. The correct way is to spoon it from the bag into a measuring cup with a spoon, and then level it with a spatula, pushing the extra back into the bag. But what a lot of people do is level it by tapping the measuring cup on the counter. That compresses the flour and you get more than you think.

Mocha White Chocolate Pecan Cookies

These cookies have a double dose of chocolate, both from the cocoa in the dough and the punctuation of white chocolate chips, plus a bit of coffee flavor for extra interest.

Yield: 2½ dozen

Active time: 15 minutes

Start to finish: 40 minutes

½ cup coarsely chopped pecans

1½ teaspoons egg replacement powder, such as Ener-G

¼ cup soy milk

1 tablespoon instant espresso powder

½ cup vegetable oil

1 teaspoon pure vanilla extract

1 cup all-purpose flour

½ cup whole-wheat pastry flour

½ cup unsweetened cocoa powder

¾ teaspoon baking powder

¼ teaspoon salt

¾ cup vegan white chocolate chips

1. Preheat the oven to 350°F. Line two baking sheets with parchment paper or silicone baking mats. Place pecans on a baking sheet, and toast for 5 to 7 minutes, or until lightly browned. Set aside.

2. Mix egg replacement powder with 2 tablespoons cold water, and set aside. Combine soy milk and espresso powder in a small microwave-safe cup, and stir well. Microwave on High (100 percent power) in 30 second intervals until coffee dissolves. Set aside to cool for 5 minutes.

3. Combine oil, egg replacement mixture, coffee mixture, and vanilla in a mixing bowl, and whisk well. Stir in all-purpose flour, whole-wheat flour, cocoa powder, baking powder, and salt. Beat at medium speed with an electric mixer until dough forms. Stir in white chocolate chips and toasted pecans.

4. Drop dough by tablespoons onto the prepared baking sheets, 1½ inches apart. Bake cookies for 12 to 15 minutes, or until browned. Allow cookies to cool for 2 minutes on the baking sheets, and then transfer cookies to racks to cool completely.

Note: Keep cookies in an airtight container, layered between sheets of waxed paper or parchment, at room temperature for up to 5 days. Cookies can also be frozen for up to 2 months.

Variations:

✳ *Substitute blanched almonds for the pecans, and substitute almond extract for the vanilla extract.*

✳ *Omit the espresso powder, and substitute dark chocolate chips for the white chocolate chips.*

✳ *Omit the espresso powder, substitute chopped almonds for the pecans, and add ½ teaspoon ground cinnamon.*

Actually ivory in color, white chocolate is technically not chocolate at all; it is made from cocoa butter, sugar, and flavoring. There are many good vegan ones on the market. It is difficult to work with, and should be used in recipes that are specifically designed for it. While other chocolate can be substituted for it, do not use white chocolate in lieu of dark chocolate in baking.

CHAPTER 4:

Bar Cookies and Brownies

There's no question that bar cookies are the quickest and easiest cookies to make. After the batter or dough is mixed it's baked in one pan and then cut into pieces. You're done. How many cookies each batch makes depends on how large the pieces are that you cut, and for Christmas when you're baking any number of different cookies, I suggest making the bars no more than $1\,^1/_2$-inch pieces.

One downside of bar cookies at Christmas, however, is that they usually don't have the visual appeal of decorated sugar cookies or whimsical gingerbread people. My suggestion is to cut them into very small bites and present them in small paper cups as miniatures. This approach also increases the batch size from twelve or sixteen larger cookies to at least two dozen.

Another way to dress them up is by cutting them into shapes other than squares and rectangles. Diamond-shaped cookies are pretty, and if you cut the bars with a round biscuit cutter you have all the tiny bits between the cookies as a treat for the cook!

A subset of bar cookies is ever-popular brownies and their first cousin, blondies. You'll find a good range of those recipes in this chapter too.

Portioning Up and Down

In addition to all their other attributes, bar cookies and brownies are easy recipes to scale up or divide down to suit your personal preference. My guess is that around the holidays making more is of more interest than making less.

If a cookie has a crust on the bottom, what is important to determine is the square inches needed. For example, an 8 x 8-inch pan creates 64 square inches, and a 9 x 13-inch pan creates 117 square inches, almost double. All that is needed is to double the recipe, and leave a tiny bit out of the pan. Do the same on the topping.

With batters it's easier to think about volume rather than square inches. Use this chart as a guide to calculating the amounts of your ingredients, and then consult a recipe that uses the pan size selected to determine the baking time and temperature.

Cake Pan Volume

8 x 8 x 2 inches:	6 cups
9 x 9 x 1½ inches:	8 cups
9 x 9 x 2 inches:	10 cups
9 x 13 x 2 inches:	14 cups

Slicing and Dicing Tips

How and when you cut bar cookies depends on the recipe. With most you allow the pan to cool completely on a wire cooling rack, and then cut them, but there are also recipes that benefit from being chilled before being sliced.

The key to successful slicing is the word *slowly*. If you cut cookies too quickly it can cause the edges to fracture and you're left with crumbs instead of slices.

If slicing them in the pan, begin by creating space in the pan by removing the four edges, which are never as attractive. Cut around about ½ inch into the pan, and then remove those thin slices and consider them a treat. Then work from alternate sides. Depending on the cookie, it's frequently easier to cut a long slice and then divide it out of the pan.

Alternate tools for successfully slicing bar cookies are a curved pizza rocker, or a traditional pizza wheel. Only use the wheel on thin cookies, but the rounded edge of the rocker makes it perfect for all cookies and brownies.

Guava Bars

I love discovering new uses for ingredients, and guava paste became my passion last year. It adds an intense fruity flavor and bright holiday red color to these chewy bar cookies.

Yield: 2 dozen

Active time: 15 minutes

Start to finish: 1 hour

10 tablespoons vegetable oil, divided

¼ cup confectioners' sugar

1¼ cups whole-wheat pastry flour, divided

Pinch of salt

1 tablespoon egg replacement powder, such as Ener-G

1 (14-ounce) block guava paste, cut into ¾-inch cubes

2 tablespoons freshly squeezed lemon juice

½ cup rolled oats

¼ cup chopped pecans (optional)

1. Preheat the oven to 350°F, and grease a 9 x 9-inch baking pan.

2. Combine ½ cup oil, confectioners' sugar, 1 cup flour, and salt in a mixing bowl, and mix thoroughly with a wooden spoon. Press mixture into the prepared pan. Bake for 20 minutes, or until set and lightly brown. Remove crust from the oven, and set aside.

3. Mix egg replacement powder with 3 tablespoons cold water, and set aside. Combine egg replacement mixture, guava paste, lemon juice, and 2 tablespoons flour in a food processor fitted with the steel blade or in a blender. Process until smooth.

4. Combine remaining oil, remaining flour, oats, and pecans, if using, in a small mixing bowl. Mix well. Spread topping over crust, and pat on oat mixture. Bake for 20 minutes, or until oats are brown. The custard should still be soft. Cool the pan on a cooling rack, then cut into squares or bars.

Note: The cookies can be refrigerated for up to 1 week, tightly covered.

Variation:
* *Add 1 teaspoon apple pie spice to the dough for a spicy bar.*

Guava paste is an inexpensive ingredient found in the Hispanic food aisle of supermarkets. It's a very thickened puree of this sweet and tart tropical fruit, and for a quick treat cut small cubes of it in granulated sugar and it has the texture and flavor of a French *pâte de fruits*.

Candied Fruit Bars

These are truly a Christmas cookie bar. They're topped with candied fruit that adds visual appeal and texture as well as flavor.

Yield: 3 to 4 dozen

Active time: 15 minutes

Start to finish: 50 minutes

1 tablespoon egg replacement powder, such as Ener-G

⅔ cup peanut oil

1½ cups firmly packed light brown sugar

½ teaspoon pure vanilla extract

1½ teaspoons baking powder

½ teaspoon salt

1⅓ cups all-purpose flour

1 cup whole-wheat pastry flour

1 cup chopped candied fruits

1. Preheat the oven to 350°F, and grease a 9 x 13-inch baking pan.

2. Mix egg replacement powder with ¼ cup cold water, and set aside. Combine oil and sugar in a saucepan. Place over medium heat and cook, stirring frequently, until sugar dissolves and mixture is smooth. Scrape mixture into a mixing bowl. Cool to room temperature.

3. Whisk egg replacement mixture and vanilla into the mixing bowl, beating until smooth. Beat in baking powder and salt, and then all-purpose and whole-wheat flours.

4. Scrape batter into the prepared pan, and pat the candied fruit evenly over the top. Bake for 20 minutes, or until a toothpick inserted in the center comes out clean. Cool the pan on a cooling rack, and then cut into bars.

Note: Keep cookies in an airtight container, layered between sheets of waxed paper or parchment, at room temperature for up to 5 days. Cookies can also be frozen for up to 2 months.

Variations:

✳ *Substitute dried cherries, dried cranberries, or chopped dried strawberries for the candied fruit.*

✳ *Substitute almond extract for the vanilla extract.*

> **Brown sugar is granulated sugar mixed with molasses, and the darker the color, the more pronounced the molasses flavor. If a recipe calls for dark brown sugar and you only have light brown sugar, add 2 tablespoons molasses per ½ cup sugar to replicate the taste.**

Peanut Butter and Jelly Bars

These bars join two favorite foods and turn them into a luscious treat rather than a sandwich. They are crunchy both from the peanut butter and the additional peanuts folded into the dough.

Yield: 1½ dozen

Active time: 15 minutes

Start to finish: 40 minutes

1½ teaspoons egg replacement powder, such as Ener-G

1 cup seedless raspberry jam

½ cup (8 tablespoons) soy margarine, softened

¾ cup commercial chunky peanut butter

¾ cup firmly packed light brown sugar

½ teaspoon pure vanilla extract

½ teaspoon baking powder

¼ teaspoon salt

1½ cups whole-wheat pastry flour

¾ cup chopped roasted peanuts

1. Preheat the oven to 350°F. Line the bottom and sides of an 8 x 8-inch baking pan with parchment paper or foil, allowing the paper to extend 2 inches over the top of the pan. Grease the paper.

2. Combine egg replacement powder and 2 tablespoons cold water, and set aside. Place jam in a saucepan and bring to a boil over medium heat, stirring frequently. Reduce the heat to low and simmer jam until reduced by one-fourth. Set aside.

3. Combine margarine, peanut butter, and sugar in a mixing bowl, and beat at low speed with an electric mixer to blend. Increase the speed to high, and beat for 3 to 4 minutes, or until light and fluffy. Beat in egg replacement mixture, vanilla, baking powder, and salt and beat for 1 minute. Slowly add flour to margarine mixture, and beat until soft dough forms. Stir in peanuts.

4. Pat ⅔ of dough into the bottom of the prepared pan. Make dollops with jam, and spread evenly over crust. Break remaining dough into 1-tablespoon pieces, flatten between your hands, and arrange on top of jam.

5. Bake bars for 25 to 30 minutes, or until top is golden brown. Cool completely on a wire rack. Lift up the ends of the parchment or foil liner, transfer brownies to a cutting board, and cut into pieces.

Note: The brownies can be made up to 3 days in advance and kept at room temperature in an airtight container.

Variations:
* *Substitute commercial almond butter for the peanut butter and chopped roasted almonds for the peanuts.*
* *Substitute apricot or peach jam for the raspberry jam.*

Peanuts are used in cuisines around the world, but peanut butter is a home-grown American invention. It was developed in 1890 and first promoted as a health food at the 1904 World's Fair in St. Louis. Pairing it with jelly on bread is a purely American treat.

Coconut Apricot Almond Bars

The crust for these delicious bars is made in the food processor so they can be in the oven in a matter of minutes. The sweet apricot jam is complemented by both the coconut and crunchy nuts.

Yield: 4 dozen

Active time: 15 minutes

Start to finish: 40 minutes

1½ cups flaked sweetened coconut, divided

1 cup whole-wheat pastry flour

½ cup all-purpose flour

1 cup firmly packed light brown sugar

¼ teaspoon salt

¾ cup (12 tablespoons) soy margarine, sliced

1 cup old-fashioned oats

¾ cup apricot preserves

¾ cup almonds in the skin

1. Preheat the oven to 375°F. Grease a 9 x 13-inch baking pan. Toast ¾ cup coconut for 6 to 8 minutes, or until golden. Set aside.

2. Combine whole-wheat and all-purpose flours, sugar, and salt in a food processor fitted with the steel blade. Blend for 5 seconds. Add margarine to the work bowl, and process until mixture resembles coarse meal. Transfer mixture to a mixing bowl, and knead in toasted coconut and oats.

3. Reserve ¾ cup dough. Press remaining dough into the bottom of the prepared pan. Spread dough with preserves. Crumble reserved dough over jam, and sprinkle with remaining coconut. Arrange almonds on top in a decorative pattern.

4. Bake for 20 to 25 minutes, or until golden. Cool the pan on a cooling rack, and then cut into bars.

Note: Keep cookies in an airtight container, layered between sheets of waxed paper or parchment, at room temperature for up to 5 days. Cookies can also be frozen for up to 2 months.

Variation:
✳ *Substitute macadamia nuts for the almonds, and substitute pineapple preserves for the apricot preserves.*

Apricots were known in Armenia during ancient times, and their Latin name, *Prunus armeniaca*, comes from that association. While cultivars have now spread all over the world, the apricot season is short, which is why apricots became one of the first fruits to go into large-scale production in their dried state.

Sesame Bars

One of my favorite candies is Middle Eastern halvah, made from ground sesame seeds, so I decided to design a cookie with a similar sweet sesame flavor, and here it is.

Yield: 4 dozen

Active time: 15 minutes

Start to finish: 40 minutes

1 cup (16 tablespoons) soy margarine

1 cup firmly packed light brown sugar

⅔ cup tahini

¼ cup silken tofu

1 teaspoon pure vanilla extract

¼ teaspoon salt

2 cups whole-wheat pastry flour

¾ cup sesame seeds

1. Preheat the oven to 350°F. Grease a 9 x 13-inch baking pan.

2. Combine margarine and sugar in a mixing bowl, and beat at low speed with an electric mixer to blend. Increase the speed to high, and beat for 3 to 4 minutes, or until light and fluffy. Beat in tahini, tofu, vanilla, and salt and beat for 1 minute. Slowly add flour to the margarine mixture, and beat until soft dough forms.

3. Spread batter evenly in the prepared pan, and top with sesame seeds, patting them down gently into dough. Bake for 18 to 20 minutes, or until seeds are golden. Cool the pan on a cooling rack, and then cut into bars.

Note: Keep cookies in an airtight container, layered between sheets of waxed paper or parchment, at room temperature for up to 5 days. Cookies can also be frozen for up to 2 months.

Variation:
✳ *Add ¾ cup dried apricots and ½ teaspoon ground ginger to the dough.*

> **We associate tahini, a paste made from hulled and lightly roasted sesame seeds, with savory dishes rather than sweet. Along with garbanzo beans, it's a main ingredient in hummus. Tahini always separates with the sesame oil on the top, regardless of the brand. Always stir it well before measuring it.**

Caramel Cashew Bars

I think cashews have a wonderful flavor, yet they're not used as frequently in baking as pecans or walnuts. These bars are rich and gooey, almost like a nut pie.

Yield: 2 dozen

Active time: 20 minutes

Start to finish: 1 hour

1½ teaspoons egg replacement powder, such as Ener-G

1 cup whole-wheat pastry flour

⅓ cup confectioners' sugar

¼ teaspoon salt

1 cup (16 tablespoons) soy margarine, divided

½ teaspoon pure vanilla extract

¼ teaspoon pure almond extract

¾ cup firmly packed light brown sugar

¼ cup light corn syrup

¼ cup silken tofu

½ pound coarsely chopped roasted unsalted cashew nuts

Soy milk or almond milk (optional), in case dough is dry

1. Preheat the oven to 375°F. Line a 9 x 9-inch baking pan with heavy-duty aluminum foil, allowing the sides to be long and wrapped around the sides of the pan. Grease the foil.

2. Mix egg replacement powder with 2 tablespoons cold water, and set aside. Combine flour, confectioners' sugar, and salt in a food processor fitted with the steel blade. Blend for 5 seconds. Add 8 tablespoons margarine to the work bowl, and process, using on-and-off pulsing, until mixture resembles coarse meal.

3. Combine egg replacement mixture, vanilla, and almond extract in a small cup, and whisk well. Drizzle liquid into the work bowl, and pulse about 10 times, or until stiff dough forms. If dough is dry and doesn't come together add soy milk or almond milk by 1-teaspoon amounts until dough forms a ball.

4. Transfer dough to the prepared pan. Using floured fingers and an offset spatula, press dough firmly into the bottom and ¾ inch up sides. Freeze until firm, about 15 minutes. Prick dough on the bottom of the pan with the tines of a fork. Bake crust for 10 to 12 minutes, or until lightly browned.

5. While crust bakes, prepare topping. Combine remaining margarine, brown sugar, and corn syrup in a saucepan, and bring to a boil over high heat, whisking constantly. Boil for 2 minutes. Remove the pan from the heat, and stir in tofu and cashews.

6. Spoon topping over crust, smoothing the top with a spatula. Bake for 20 to 22 minutes, or until topping is bubbling and dark brown. Cool completely in the pan on a cooling rack. Remove cookies from the pan by pulling up on the sides of the foil, and cut into bars.

Note: Keep cookies in an airtight container, layered between sheets of waxed paper or parchment, at room temperature for up to 5 days.

Variations:
* *Substitute maple sugar for the light brown sugar, substitute pure maple syrup for the corn syrup, and substitute walnuts for the cashews.*
* *Add ½ cup dried currants or chopped dried figs to the topping.*

Almond Bars

Almond paste is really nothing more complicated than almonds ground with sugar and given a more intense flavor with almond extract; it is almost a "convenience food." That means these delicious bars are quick to make too.

Yield: 2 dozen

Active time: 15 minutes

Start to finish: 1 hour

1½ teaspoons egg replacement powder, such as Ener-G

1¼ cups whole-wheat pastry flour

¾ cup confectioners' sugar

½ teaspoon baking soda

¼ teaspoon salt

¾ cup (12 tablespoons) soy margarine, sliced

1 (7-ounce) tube almond paste, crumbled

1 tablespoon almond milk

1 teaspoon pure almond extract

1 tablespoon powdered agar

1 cup sliced unbalanced almonds

1. Preheat the oven to 350ºF. Grease a 9 x 9-inch baking pan.

2. Mix egg replacement powder with 2 tablespoons cold water, and set aside. Combine flour, confectioners' sugar, baking soda, and salt in a food processor fitted with the steel blade. Blend for 5 seconds. Add margarine and almond paste to the work bowl, and process until mixture resembles coarse meal.

3. Combine egg replacement mixture, almond milk, and almond extract in a small cup, and stir well. Drizzle liquid into the work bowl, and pulse about 10 times, or until stiff dough forms. If dough is dry and doesn't come together, add additional almond milk by 1-teaspoon amounts, until dough forms a ball.

4. Press dough into the prepared pan. Stir agar powder and 1 tablespoon cold water in a small cup and spread over dough. Pat almonds evenly onto dough.

5. Bake for 35 to 40 minutes, or until top is golden. Cool completely in the pan on a cooling rack, then cut into bars.

Note: Keep cookies in an airtight container, layered between sheets of waxed paper or parchment, at room temperature for up to 5 days. Cookies can also be frozen for up to 2 months.

Variations:
* Substitute chocolate chips for the almonds, and omit the agar powder wash.
* Add ½ cup finely chopped dried apricots or dried currants to the dough.

> **Make sure when you're in the market that you buy almond paste and not marzipan. They usually have them right next to each other on the shelf. While marzipan has an almond flavor, it already has sugar added.**

Baklava

Baklava is a wonderful layered Greek and Middle Eastern pastry that is baked and then soaked in a sweet syrup. Although it does take some time to assemble, the recipe makes a large batch, and your guests will adore it.

Yield: 4 to 5 dozen

Active time: 40 minutes

Start to finish: 1½ hours

3½ cups walnuts

½ cup granulated sugar

1 teaspoon ground cinnamon

¼ teaspoon ground cloves

1 (1-pound) package vegan phyllo sheets, such as Fillo Factory, thawed

1½ cups (24 tablespoons) soy margarine, melted

2 cups firmly packed light brown sugar

1 lemon, seeded and thinly sliced

1 (3-inch) cinnamon stick

1. Preheat the oven to 350°F. Place walnuts on a baking sheet, and toast for 5 to 7 minutes, or until lightly browned. Remove the pan from the oven, and combine nuts, ½ cup sugar, cinnamon, and cloves in a food processor fitted with the steel blade. Chop very finely using on-and-off pulsing, or by hand.

2. Increase the oven temperature to 375ºF, and grease a 12 x 16-inch rimmed baking sheet pan. Place phyllo on a plate, and cover it with plastic wrap or a damp paper towel to keep it from drying out.

3. Place 1 sheet of phyllo in the baking pan, and brush with melted margarine. Repeat with 7 other sheets, and sprinkle with ⅓ of nut mixture. Place 4 more sheets of phyllo on top of nut mixture, brushing each with margarine. Sprinkle with ⅓ of nut mixture, and then repeat. Top last round of nut mixture with remaining sheets of phyllo, brushing each, including the top one, with margarine. Trim edges to make a neat rectangle.

4. Cut pastry into 2-inch squares or triangles through the three nut layers. Do not cut through the bottom crust. Bake for 25 to 30 minutes, or until the top layer of phyllo is brown.

5. Prepare syrup while pastry bakes. Combine brown sugar, 1½ cups water, lemon, and cinnamon stick in a saucepan. Bring to a boil over medium heat, stirring occasionally. Reduce the heat to low, and simmer syrup for 10 minutes. Strain syrup, and keep hot.

6. Remove the pan from the oven and immediately pour hot syrup over the baklava. Place pan on a cooling rack, and cool to room temperature. Cut through bottom layer of crust once cooled.

Note: Keep cookies in an airtight container, layered between sheets of waxed paper or parchment, at room temperature for up to 5 days.

Variation:
* *Substitute pecans, macadamia nuts, or almonds for the walnuts.*

> **Pastry brushes are expensive, but paintbrushes are cheap. Any natural-bristle paintbrush can be used as a pastry brush. But don't use a foam rubber brush; those are not safe for food preparation.**

Almond Chocolate Blondies

Blondies came about when folks wanted to figure out a way to bake chocolate chip cookies as bar cookies. Here's a more sophisticated version because it includes almonds too.

Yield: 3 to 4 dozen

Active time: 15 minutes

Start to finish: 1 hour

1 tablespoon egg replacement powder, such as Ener-G

⅔ cup peanut oil

1½ cups firmly packed light brown sugar

½ teaspoon pure almond extract

1½ teaspoons baking powder

½ teaspoon salt

1⅓ cups all-purpose flour

1 cup whole-wheat pastry flour

¾ cup vegan bittersweet chocolate chips

½ cup sliced almonds

1. Preheat the oven to 350°F, and grease a 9 x 13-inch baking pan.

2. Mix egg replacement powder with ¼ cup cold water, and set aside. Combine oil and sugar in a saucepan. Place over medium heat and cook, stirring frequently, until sugar dissolves and mixture is smooth. Scrape mixture into a mixing bowl. Cool to room temperature.

3. Whisk egg replacement mixture and almond extract into the mixing bowl, beating until smooth. Beat in baking powder and salt, and then all-purpose and whole-wheat flours. Fold in chocolate chips.

4. Scrape batter into the pan, and sprinkle almonds on top. Bake for 20 minutes, or until a toothpick inserted in the center comes out clean. Cool the pan on a cooling rack, and then cut into bars.

Note: Keep cookies in an airtight container, layered between sheets of waxed paper or parchment, at room temperature for up to 5 days. Cookies can also be frozen for up to 2 months.

Variation:
✳ *Substitute vegan white chocolate chips for the bittersweet chips, vanilla for the almond extract, and pecans for the almonds.*

When you're testing a baked good with a toothpick, always use a wooden toothpick. The purpose of the test is to determine if the center is still raw, and plastic toothpicks will slip in and out without having any telltale crumbs hanging.

Chocolate Walnut Brownies

Brownies don't get any more deeply flavored than this, and the crunchy nuts both in the batter and baked on the top add a textural contrast to the fudgy flavor.

Yield: 2 dozen

Active time: 15 minutes

Start to finish: 1 hour

1 tablespoon egg replacement powder, such as Ener-G

1 cup coarsely chopped walnuts, divided

⅔ cup (10 tablespoons) soy margarine, sliced

1 cup granulated sugar

¼ cup firmly packed light brown sugar

1 cup unsweetened cocoa powder (natural or Dutch-process)

¼ teaspoon salt

½ teaspoon pure vanilla extract

½ cup whole-wheat pastry flour

1. Preheat the oven to 350°F. Line the bottom and sides of an 8 x 8-inch baking pan with parchment paper or foil, allowing the paper to extend 2 inches over the top of the pan. Grease the paper. Mix egg replacement powder with ¼ cup cold water, and set aside.

2. Toast ½ cup walnuts for 5 to 7 minutes, or until browned. Remove nuts from the oven, and reduce the oven temperature to 325°F.

3. Combine margarine, granulated sugar, brown sugar, cocoa, and salt in a medium heatproof bowl and set the bowl in a wide skillet of barely simmering water. Whisk it from time to time until margarine melts and mixture is smooth and hot. Remove the bowl from the skillet and set aside briefly until the mixture is only warm, not hot.

4. Stir in vanilla and eggs replacement mixture, and whisk until looks thick and shiny. Add flour, and whisk until incorporated, and then beat for 1 minute with a spoon. Stir in toasted nuts, and spread batter evenly in the prepared pan. Top with untoasted nuts.

5. Bake in the center of the oven for 20 to 25 minutes, or until a toothpick inserted into the center comes out with just a few crumbs attached. Cool completely on a wire rack. Lift up the ends of the parchment or foil liner, transfer brownies to a cutting board, and cut into pieces.

Note: The brownies can be made up to 3 days in advance and kept at room temperature in an airtight container.

Variations:
* *Substitute pure orange oil for the vanilla, and add 2 tablespoons grated orange zest to the batter.*
* *For mocha brownies, stir 1 tablespoon instant espresso powder to the egg replacement mixture.*

Cocoa powder should be stored in a cool, dark place, but not in the refrigerator because the humidity can promote spoilage. Because of its low moisture content, cocoa powder will keep up to three years.

Mocha Spice Brownies

There's a lot going on in these complexly flavored brownies. In addition to the time-honored tradition of joining chocolate and coffee, some spice is added to enliven the taste buds even more.

Yield: 2 dozen

Active time: 15 minutes

Start to finish: 45 minutes

Unsweetened cocoa powder for dusting

1 tablespoon egg replacement powder, such as Ener-G

3 ounces unsweetened baking chocolate, chopped

½ cup vegetable oil

1 cup granulated sugar

¼ cup firmly packed light brown sugar

2 tablespoons instant espresso powder

2 tablespoons Kahlúa, or other coffee-flavored liqueur

½ teaspoon baking powder

½ teaspoon Chinese five-spice powder

¼ teaspoon salt

¾ cup whole-wheat pastry flour

5 ounces bittersweet chocolate, chopped

3 tablespoons soy margarine, sliced

1. Preheat the oven to 350°F. Grease a 9 x 9-inch baking pan, and dust it with cocoa powder, knocking out any excess.

2. Mix egg replacement powder with 2 tablespoons cold water, and set aside. Combine chocolate with oil in a microwave safe bowl. Microwave on Medium (50 percent power) at 30 second intervals, stirring between intervals, until chocolate is melted and smooth. Set aside for 5 minutes to cool.

3. Add egg replacement mixture, granulated sugar, brown sugar, espresso powder, liqueur, baking powder, five-spice powder, and salt into cooled chocolate. Beat at medium speed with an electric mixer for 1 minute. Beat in flour at low speed.

4. Scrape batter into the prepared pan, and spread evenly. Bake for 30 to 35 minutes, or until a wooden toothpick inserted into the center comes out with just a few crumbs attached. Cool completely on a wire rack.

5. Combine bittersweet chocolate and margarine in a small saucepan, and melt over low heat. Stir until smooth. Place dollops of chocolate on top of brownies, and spread gently to cover.

6. Chill brownies, lightly covered with plastic wrap, for at least 1 hour, or until chocolate is firm. Brownies can be refrigerated for up to 3 days. Cut into pieces. Bring to room temperature before serving.

Note: Keep brownies in an airtight container, layered between sheets of waxed paper or parchment, at room temperature for up to 5 days.

Variation:
* *Omit the Chinese five-spice powder and add 2 tablespoons additional cocoa to the batter.*

The purpose of dusting a pan with flour before baking is to make it easier to remove the brownies or cake. But if you're making a chocolate dessert that does not get frosting, it's better to dust the pan with additional cocoa powder. It will look prettier, and it will just add to the chocolate flavor.

Chocolate Peanut Brownies

Rich and creamy peanut butter frosting tops the base layer and then there's an additional dose of chocolate on top. For anyone who loves the combination of chocolate and peanuts, this recipe is heaven.

Yield: 2 dozen

Active time: 25 minutes

Start to finish: 2 hours

8 ounces chopped bittersweet chocolate, divided

⅓ cup vegetable oil

1 cup granulated sugar

1½ teaspoons pure vanilla extract, divided

½ cup soy milk, divided

1½ cups whole-wheat pastry flour

½ cup unsweetened cocoa powder

1½ teaspoons baking powder

1 cup roasted salted peanuts, coarsely chopped

¾ cup chunky commercial peanut butter (do not use natural)

6 tablespoons soy margarine, softened, divided

¾ cup confectioners' sugar

1. Preheat the oven to 350°F. Line the bottom and sides of an 9 x 9-inch baking pan with parchment paper or foil, allowing the paper to extend 2 inches over the top of the pan. Grease the paper.

2. Combine 3 ounces chocolate and oil in a microwave safe bowl. Microwave on Medium (50 percent power) at 30-second intervals, stirring between intervals, until chocolate is melted and smooth. Scrape into a mixing bowl, and set aside for 5 minutes to cool.

3. Reserve 1 tablespoon soy milk. Add sugar, 1 teaspoon vanilla, and remaining soy milk to the mixing bowl. Whisk until smooth. Combine flour, cocoa powder, and baking powder, and whisk well. Add flour mixture to the liquids, and whisk until smooth. Stir in peanuts.

4. Scrape batter into the prepared pan, and smooth the top with a spatula. Bake for 20 to 23 minutes, or until a toothpick inserted into the center comes out with just a few moist crumbs attached. Cool completely in the pan on a cooling rack.

5. Combine peanut butter and margarine in a mixing bowl, and beat at low speed with an electric mixer to combine. Add confectioners' sugar, reserved soy milk, and remaining vanilla, and beat for 2 minutes, or until light and fluffy. Spread mixture on top of brownies, and chill brownies for 1 hour.

6. Combine remaining chocolate and remaining margarine in a small saucepan, and melt over low heat. Stir until smooth. Place dollops of chocolate on top of peanut butter layer, and spread gently to cover peanut butter layer completely.

7. Chill brownies, lightly covered with plastic wrap, for at least 1 hour, or until chocolate is firm. Brownies can be refrigerated for up to 3 days. Remove brownies from the pan by pulling up on the sides of the foil. Cut into pieces. Bring to room temperature before serving.

Note: Keep brownies in an airtight container, layered between sheets of waxed paper or parchment, refrigerated, for up to 3 days.

Variation:
✻ *Substitute commercial almond butter and almonds for the peanut butter and peanuts.*

Chocolate Orange Walnut Brownies

While chocolate has an assertive flavor it also pairs well with so many other tastes— orange being one of my favorites. These brownies containing chopped candied orange peel are truly delicious.

Yield: 2 dozen

Active time: 15 minutes

Start to finish: 1 hour

1 tablespoon egg replacement powder, such as Ener-G

¾ cup coarsely chopped walnuts

10 tablespoons (1¼ sticks) soy margarine, softened

1 cup granulated sugar

¼ cup firmly packed light brown sugar

1 cup unsweetened cocoa powder (natural or Dutch-process)

¼ teaspoon salt

½ teaspoon pure orange oil

½ cup all-purpose flour

¼ cup finely chopped candied orange peel

1. Preheat the oven to 350°F. Line the bottom and sides of an 8 x 8-inch baking pan with parchment paper or foil, allowing the paper to extend 2 inches over the top of the pan. Grease the paper. Mix egg replacement powder with ¼ cup cold water, and set aside.

2. Toast walnuts for 5 to 7 minutes, or until browned. Remove nuts from the oven, and reduce the oven temperature to 325 degrees.

3. Combine margarine, granulated sugar, brown sugar, cocoa, and salt in a medium heatproof bowl and set the bowl in a wide skillet of barely simmering water. Whisk it from time to time until margarine melts and mixture is smooth and hot. Remove the bowl from the skillet and set aside briefly until the mixture is only warm, not hot.

4. Stir in orange oil and eggs replacement mixture, and whisk until looks thick and shiny. Add flour, and whisk until incorporated, and then beat for 1 minute with a spoon. Stir in toasted nuts and orange peel, and spread batter evenly in the prepared pan. Top with untoasted nuts.

5. Bake in the center of the oven for 20 to 25 minutes, or until a wooden toothpick inserted into the center comes out with just a few crumbs attached. Cool completely on a wire rack. Lift up the ends of the parchment or foil liner, transfer brownies to a cutting board, and cut into pieces.

Note: The brownies can be made up to 3 days in advance and kept at room temperature in an airtight container.

Variation:
✳ *Substitute vanilla for the orange extract and substitute chopped candied fruit for the candied orange peel.*

There are two types of cocoa on the market, natural and Dutch-process. Dutch-process cocoa powder has an extra step in the production process. Before the shelled beans are ground, they are soaked in an alkaline solution to neutralize their natural acidity. This removes any bitter or sour flavors in the cocoa and also turns it a darker color than natural cocoa powder.

Chocolate Peppermint Brownies

Most people associate fresh-tasting mint with the holidays, but I make these rich and chewy brownies during all seasons. The flavor combination of chocolate with mint is a natural, which is why Peppermint Patties have been a candy beloved for generations.

Yield: 2 to 3 dozen miniatures

Active time: 15 minutes

Start to finish: 1 hour

1 tablespoon egg replacement powder, such as Ener-G

3 ounces bittersweet chocolate, chopped

1 cup (16 tablespoons) soy margarine, softened, divided

1 cup all-purpose flour

3 tablespoons unsweetened cocoa powder

½ teaspoon salt

2½ cups confectioners' sugar, divided

½ teaspoon pure vanilla extract

2 tablespoons soy milk

½ to 1 teaspoon mint oil

2 to 4 drops green food coloring (optional)

¾ cup crushed bittersweet chocolate

1. Preheat the oven to 350ºF, and grease 9 x 9-inch baking pan.

2. Mix egg replacement powder with 2 tablespoons cold water, and set aside. Combine chocolate and 4 tablespoons margarine in a microwave-safe bowl. Microwave on Medium (50 percent power) at 30-second intervals, stirring between intervals, until chocolate is melted and smooth. Set aside. Combine flour, cocoa powder, and salt in a mixing bowl. Whisk well.

3. Combine 8 tablespoons margarine and ½ cup sugar in another mixing bowl and beat at low speed with an electric mixer to blend. Increase the speed to high, and beat for 3 to 4 minutes, or until light and fluffy. Add egg replacement mixture, cooled chocolate, and vanilla. Slowly add dry ingredients to the butter mixture, and beat well.

4. Scrape batter into the prepared pan, and spread evenly. Bake for 18 to 20 minutes, or until a toothpick inserted into the center comes out clean. Cool completely in the pan on a cooling rack.

5. For frosting, combine remaining margarine, remaining sugar, and soy milk in a mixing bowl. Beat at medium speed with an electric mixer until light and fluffy. Add mint oil and green food coloring, if using, and beat well. Add additional soy milk by 1-teaspoon amounts if frosting is too thick to spread.

6. Spread frosting over brownies, and sprinkle crushed chocolate evenly over frosting. Cut into small bars.

Note: Keep brownies in an airtight container, layered between sheets of waxed paper or parchment, at room temperature for up to 5 days.

Variation:
✳ *Substitute pure almond extract for the mint oil, omit the food coloring, and substitute slivered almonds (toasted in a 350ºF oven for 7 to 9 minutes) for the peppermint candies.*
✳ *Substitute red food coloring for the green food coloring and crushed red and white peppermint candies for the crushed bittersweet chocolate.*

INDEX

About the Author

Ellen Brown is a well-respected author of more than thirty cookbooks. These include the following titles from Cider Mill Press: *The Meatball Cookbook Bible, The Sausage Cookbook Bible, Gluten-Free Holiday Cookies, Gluten-Free Slow Cooking*, and *Italian Slow Cooking. Gluten-Free Holiday Baking* will also be published in 2012.

As the founding food writer of *USA Today*, Ellen gained the national spotlight in 1982. Since then, her writing has appeared in dozens of publications, including *The Washington Post, Bon Appetit*, and *Good Food Dossier*.

Ellen lives in Providence, Rhode Island, and writes a weekly column for *The Providence Journal* featuring a range of original recipes.

About Cider Mill Press Book Publishers

Good ideas ripen with time. From seed to harvest, Cider Mill Press brings fine reading, information, and entertainment together between the covers of its creatively crafted books. Our Cider Mill bears fruit twice a year, publishing a new crop of titles each spring and fall.

Visit us on the Web at
www.cidermillpress.com
or write to us at
12 Port Farm Road
Kennebunkport, Maine 04046